BETWEEN THE WARS

צווישן צוויי
וועלט מלחמות

פון י. מדרש

מאָנטרעאָל — 1964   "קענעדער אדלער" דרוקעריי

[Title page, original Yiddish edition, 1964]

Between the Wars

CANADIAN JEWS IN TRANSITION

Israel Medres

TRANSLATED FROM THE YIDDISH BY

Vivian Felsen

Véhicule Press

Published and translated with the generous assistance of The Canada Council
for the Arts, the Book Publishing Industry Development Program of the Department of Canadian Heritage, and the Société de développement des entreprises
culturelles du Québec (SODEC).

Cover design: JW Stewart
Set in Adobe Minion by Simon Garamond
Printed by AGMV-Marquis Inc.

This translation is based on *Tsvishn Tsvey Velt Milkhomes,*
Eagle Publishing Co. Ltd., 1964, with the permission of the
Estate of Israel Medres.

CATALOGUING IN PUBLICATION DATA

Medres, Israel, 1894-1964
Between the wars : Canadian Jews in transition /
Israel Medres ; translated from the Yiddish by
Vivian Felsen

Translation of Tsvishn Tsvey Velt Milkhomes.

Includes biographical references and index.
ISBN 1-55065-174-9

1. Jews–Quebec (Province)–Montréal–20th century.
2. Jews–Quebec (Province)–Politics and government–20th century.
3. Antisemitism–Quebec (Province)–History–20th century.
4. Canadian Jewish Congress–History. I. Title.

FC2947.9.J4M4413 2003   971.4'28004924   C2003-903241-8

Véhicule Press
www.vehiculepress.com

CANADIAN DISTRIBUTION: LitDistCo Distribution, 100 Armstrong Avenue,
Georgetown, Ontario, L7G 5S4 / 800-591-6250 / orders@litdistco.ca

U.S. DISTRIBUTION: Independent Publishers Group, 814 North Franklin Street,
Chicago, Illinois 60610 / 800-888-4741 / frontdesk@ipgbook.com

Printed in Canada

Acknowledgments

As in the case of Israel Medres' first book, *Montreal of Yesterday*, The Canada Council for the Arts generously provided a translation grant to assist in making *Between the Wars* available to an English-speaking readership. In preparing the book for publication, I benefited from the knowledge and expertise of a number of people. I am especially grateful to Pierre Anctil, member of the Institut québécois sur la culture juive and translator of Medres' work into French. In addition, I wish to thank Janice Rosen, Director, Canadian Jewish Congress Archives in Montreal; Eiran Harris, Archivist, Montreal Jewish Public Library; Howard Markus, Ontario Jewish Archives; Zachary Baker, Stanford University Libraries; Peter Heichelheim; Abe Shenitzer; Beth Kaplan; and in particular my publisher Simon Dardick of Véhicule Press. My aunt and uncle, Sylvia and Phil Madras, participants in the life and times described in *Between the Wars*, took a lively interest in the entire publication process. Finally, the book was enhanced by the advice and suggestions of my husband Shim, whose good judgment has been invaluable.

Israel Medres (1894-1964), his wife Sophe Victor Medres (1891-1982), and
three of their four children: Abe Madras (1917-1998), Anne Medres
Glass (1919-1982), Samuel Madras (1915-2001).
This photograph was taken in 1922, the year Israel Medres became a
full-time staff writer for the Montreal Yiddish daily, the *Keneder Adler*.

Contents

Translator's Introduction

When *Between the Wars* was first published in its original Yiddish version in the spring of 1964, it was acclaimed in the Yiddish press as a valuable account of a turbulent and tragic time in the history of the Jews of Canada.[1] Its author, Israel Medres, was a seasoned journalist and newspaper reporter. Of special interest were descriptions of events the author himself had witnessed and interviews he had personally conducted with a variety of people, from diplomats to soldiers, from politicians to poets. *Between the Wars* was considered a source of historical treasures, and historians and social scientists would go on to mine these treasures,[2] as they had Medres' earlier writings.[3]

When the book appeared in French thirty-seven years later, translated by anthropologist and historian Pierre Anctil, it was received with equal enthusiasm by Canada's two leading French-language newspapers.[4] Despite the fact much had already been written since 1964 on the Jews of Canada during the interwar period, the reviewer in *La Presse* found important discoveries to be made in this book.[5] His opinion was echoed in *Le Devoir* where *Between the Wars* was called a document of the utmost importance.[6] For these reviewers the book offered a unique view, from the inside, of the Jewish community at a critical period in its history.

Like their Jewish colleagues in the early 1960s, the French journalists, almost four decades later, declared Israel Medres to be an ideal observer and chronicler of his times. First and foremost, he was intimately acquainted with the community he was describing. Arriving in Montreal in 1910, at the age of sixteen, Medres was typical of the tens of thousands of Yiddish-speaking Jewish immigrants who came to Canada during the first two decades of the twentieth century, fleeing the poverty, persecution, and pogroms of Eastern Europe. Once in Canada they found work mainly in factories and sweatshops, struggled to maintain their Jewish identity—their language, their traditions, and the ideologies of Zionism and socialism they had imported from Eastern Europe —and created the institutions which laid the foundations of the Jewish community in Canada as it exists today.

Israel Medres was born in 1894 in Lechovich.[7] This Byelorussian town of

120 Jewish families was situated in the Minsk *guberniia*, one of the fifteen provinces designated as the Pale of Settlement to which the majority of Jews in the Russian Empire—indeed all of Eastern Europe—were confined by law.[8] When Medres was thirteen, the family moved to the neighbouring city of Baranovich, and he was sent to the Lida Yeshiva.[9] The founder and head of the Lida Yeshiva, Rabbi Jacob Reines, was known for introducing modern methodology to the study of religious texts and for incorporating secular subjects, including mathematics and Russian, into the curriculum of his yeshiva. He was also a founder of the religious Zionist movement, the Mizrachi. This great scholar instilled in Medres a love of learning, a love of the Jewish land, and, above all, *ahavas yisroel*, a love of the Jewish people. His three years in the yeshiva provided Medres with the skills he needed to become a journalist, and gave him the world view he would retain for the rest of his life.

The oldest of several children, Israel Medres was given the opportunity to escape the harsh conditions of overcrowding and unemployment in the Pale. At sixteen he journeyed alone to the home of his mother's brother who had settled in Montreal. The rest of the family, except for one sister, remained in the old country. They were among the 6,000,000 Jews who perished in the Holocaust.

During his first twelve years in Montreal, Medres had various jobs, including loading and unloading the ships in the harbour and working as a tailor in a sweatshop. These experiences resulted in his lifelong involvement in the labour movement and explain why Medres felt so comfortable with all types of Jews and they with him—from the very religious to avowed atheists, from Bundists to Zionists, from trade unionists to Hebraist scholars, from English-speaking philanthropists to the Yiddish-speaking masses. For Medres, the ideals of social justice, equality, and freedom were completely compatible with Jewish tradition.

In 1922, Medres became a full-time staff writer for the Montreal Yiddish daily, the *Keneder Adler* (Jewish Daily Eagle). For over forty years before the publication of *Between the Wars,* Medres served the newspaper in numerous capacities, including news editor, labour editor, court reporter, and political affairs columnist. His reports of the meetings, conferences, and congresses of all the various groups and organizations in the Jewish community can be found in the pages of the *Keneder Adler,* sometimes in the English-language *Jewish Chronicle,* and in the Labour Zionist newspaper *Dos Vort,* which he edited. In addition, he was the Montreal correspondent for the Yiddish daily the *Morgn*

Zhurnal (Jewish Morning Journal) of New York. His articles were often reprinted in Yiddish papers in the United States, Mexico, South America, and Europe.

For *Between the Wars*, Medres selected what he must have considered the highlights of his countless pages of reportage, including his eyewitness accounts of the notorious anti-Jewish rallies in Montreal in the 1930s. His regular columns included *Bilder fun gericht* (Scenes from the Courtroom), which he began writing in the 1920s, *Kanader tsayt notitsen* (Canada Today) in the 1930s, *In der arbeter velt* (In The World of Labour*)* beginning in the 1940s, and *Fun montik biz montik* (From Monday to Monday) during World War II, reporting in detail the course of the war. Medres also conducted numerous interviews for the *Keneder Adler*, among them the dramatic interview with Premier Duplessis included in *Between the Wars* which the reviewer in *La Presse* considered worthy of a historical novel. He interviewed the young man at the centre of the 1934 doctors' strike against the hiring by a Montreal hospital of a Jewish intern. In the war years, with two sons overseas, Medres often visited the military bases near Montreal, interviewing young Jewish soldiers and officers. The account of his 1944 meeting with the doomed Soviet Jewish poet Itzik Feffer, sent to North America as a representative of the Soviet government, is particularly poignant.

Medres' involvement in the community extended beyond his work as a newspaperman. He was a long-time and active member of the independent Poalei Zion,[10] the socialist Zionist movement. He gave lectures to union members on labour history.[11] He was a sought-after speechwriter, and whenever an important speech was delivered in any of the Jewish organizations of Montreal in the 1940s, fifties and early sixties, members of the audience would later discuss among themselves whether it had been penned by Medres or Ginsburg.[12] Both were considered "stars" of the Yiddish press.[13] On Medres' sixtieth birthday in 1954, his colleague Joseph Gallay wrote that Medres was a "walking encyclopedia" of the Montreal Jewish community; that virtually all of Montreal knew Medres. The committee organized by the Labour Zionists to support the publication of *Between the Wars* included a prominent rabbi from the Mizrachi organization, as well as leaders of various other Jewish organizations.[14]

During Medres' lifetme, Montreal was Canada's largest city. All the Canada-wide Jewish organizations were founded and had their head offices there, including the two largest: the Canadian Jewish Congress and the Canadian

Zionist Federation. As the situation of the Jews in Europe deteriorated in the wake of World War I, the Russian Revolution, and the rise of reaction in Eastern and Central Europe, the centre of Jewish life began to shift from Europe to America, and Montreal assumed even greater importance. *Between the Wars* describes how Canadian Jews shouldered this new burden of responsibility.

As a journalist, Medres' goal was to give expression to all that united the various factions in Jewish life, rather than what divided them, and he was respected for his even-handedness. Although very soon after his arrival in Canada Medres joined the ranks of the Poalei Zion, his approach to Jewish problems was not limited by strict dogma or narrow doctrine.[15] In *Between the Wars,* without neglecting other groups in the community, Medres devotes several chapters to Zionism in its various forms. In fact, he could have placed even more emphasis on the Labour Zionists who were instrumental in the founding of many of the important institutions in Jewish life, including the Canadian Jewish Congress, the Jewish Public Library, and Jewish schools.

His ability to consider all aspects of an issue extended even to his treatment of anti-Semitism in Canada in the interwar years. In his report to the New York Yiddish daily, the *Morgn Zhurnal,* Medres quoted extensively from the response of Cardinal Villeneuve who decried the virulent anti-Semitism in Montreal during the summer of 1935.[16] Similarly, in *Between the Wars,* the chapter about the torching of the newly-constructed Quebec City synagogue by anti-Semites ends with a quote from the chairman of the building committee, Maurice Pollack, who reminded Jews "not to lose their trust in French Quebecers who were fundamentally honest, hard-working, God-fearing and hospitable people."

The parts of the book dealing with anti-Semitism in Canada in the 1930s were of particular interest to the reviewers in the Yiddish press in 1964. They took special notice of the fact that in Canada there were always Christian defenders of the Jews. *Between the Wars* provides a positive portrayal of Henri Bourrassa, "the intellectual leader of French Canadian nationalism", and other French Canadians who took steps to combat anti-Semitism, such as the journalists Olivar Asselin and Edmond Turcotte, who wrote for the Montreal daily *Le Canada,* the diplomat Raoul Dandurand, and the judge Gonzalvez Desaulniers of the Quebec Superior Court. The lengthy 1935 judgment of Mr. Justice Desaulniers condemning anti-Semitism was singled out for comment. One reviewer found it "amazing and incomprehensible" that the Canadian Jewish Congress had never disseminated the historic decision of this courageous judge in printed form, to serve in the struggle against anti-Semitism and hatred.[17] It is no wonder that when it appeared in French translation, *Between the Wars* was immediately hailed by the Montreal French-language dailies as an important book and essential reading.[18] Unfortunately, the chapters on anti-Semitism seem to have even more relevance today than they did in the 1960s, and the anti-Zionist arguments of the anti-Semites sound all too familiar.

There are significant differences between Medres' two books. The first, *Montreal of Yesterday* (published in Yiddish in 1947 as *Montreal fun nekhtn*) is a social history, dealing with the everyday lives of the early immigrants. *Between the Wars* is broader in scope, focussing more on the Canadian Jewish community as a whole, and often encompassing the entire Jewish world as Medres attempts to present events in their political and historical context. *Montreal of Yesterday* exemplified Medres' characteristic gentle sense of humour in describing a more innocent era. In *Between the Wars,* documenting the tragedies and triumphs of the twentieth century, the tone is sombre.

In his first book, Medres described an immigrant community which had brought with it the culture of the Eastern European Yiddish-speaking Jews. Here in Canada, between 1900 and 1920, that culture flourished. In his second book, Medres chronicles its decline, due in large measure to catastrophic world events which completely destroyed Jewish life in Eastern Europe. But Medres makes clear that the decline of Yiddish culture was also the result of the very success of the Canadian Jewish community. In 1964, numbering just over a quarter of a million, Canadian Jews had made tremendous strides toward equality and acceptance.

Like most other Jews in the early 1960s, Medres was optimistic about the future of the State of Israel and its positive influence on Jews worldwide. From today's perspective, it is almost painful to read about the naïve and idyllic hopes of the early Zionists that anti-Semitism would disappear once the Jews had a country of their own, and that Arab and Jew would live in harmony.

Between the Wars records the dramatic transformation of Canadian Jewry from a predominantly Yiddish-speaking, working-class, immigrant community into the English-speaking, mostly middle-class community of the 1950s. While Medres felt completely at home in Jewish Montreal with its many cultural, political, and religious currents, we sense in the final chapters of *Between the Wars* that he is becoming an outsider in the Jewish community of the early 1960s, now dominated by Canadian-born and Canadian-educated

Jews. The author's observations on the new developments in Jewish life—the flight to suburbia, the new synagogues, assimilation, and the impact of the State of Israel—are of interest precisely because of this new vantage point. They add yet another dimension to the book. His musings on what constitutes Jewish identity are still timely. These are issues that Jews around the world are still grappling with today.

Author's Preface

Jewish life in Canada, as in other countries, was profoundly affected by the turbulent, dramatic and tragic occurrences in the era between the two world wars.

It is my purpose in this book to present the developments and changes within the Jewish community in light of these historic events which transformed the entire world.

1964

The First Cataclysm

The Transformation of Europe and European Jewry in the Wake of World War I.
The Kerensky Revolt against Tsarism. The Communist Counter-Revolution.

THE TWO WORLD WARS of 1914 and 1939 brought colossal changes to all the nations of the world, but most of all to the Jewish people. The map of the Jewish world was completely redrawn. Eastern European Jewry, with its centuries-old traditions, was spiritually and culturally annihilated. A Jewish state was created in Israel, while a large Jewish population became concentrated in North America—in the United States and Canada.

During World War I, the Jewish communities of Eastern Europe, situated for the most part within the Russian Empire, had endured tremendous suffering. Yet, while the war of 1914 had inflicted terrible tragedies on these communities, they had not been obliterated. In the Second World War, the destruction was total. Large, well established communities vanished, and a unique way of life was lost. Eastern European Jewish civilization and culture, which had so profoundly influenced the spiritual and cultural life of Jews all over the world, were completely eradicated.

The tsarist regime, hostile to Jews, had enacted discriminatory laws against the Jewish population preventing them from residing in certain parts of the Russian Empire. When the war broke out, Jews were portrayed as enemies and German sympathizers. Russian generals ordered Jews expelled from all the cities and towns near the front. As the German armies advanced, the Russians retreated, and the further the Russians retreated, the greater grew the number of localities emptied of Jews.

Jews in the United States and Canada, as well as England, protested against the tsarist persecution of Jews. But since the tsar was an ally in the effort to defeat the Kaiser's armies, which had proven to be much stronger than anticipated, these protests had little effect. In democratic countries there was a great deal of sympathy for the Jews, but no one wanted a confrontation with the tsar over his anti-Semitism. Jewish leaders were merely given assurances that once the war was over and Kaiser Wilhelm defeated, the tsar would be persuaded to modify his attitude toward the Jews and grant full equality to the Jewish citizens of the Russian Empire, which then included Poland and Lithuania, home to large Jewish communities with their highly developed · Jewish spiritual and cultural life.

The war ended in a victory over the German armies, but the tsar did not live to see it. By the time the war was over, the Revolution of 19 17 had already taken place and tsarism had been completely eliminated. Bourgeois liberals under the leadership of Duma deputy Alexander Kerensky had orchestrated the first revolution against the tsar. The Kerensky revolution was welcomed by all the democracies. For Jews in the United States and Canada it signified the end of a period of Jewish disenfranchisement in Russia. There were great expectations for the future of Russian Jewry. Jews rejoiced over the fall of the tsar and the advent of democracy and liberalism to the vast Russian empire. Russian liberals had always been sympathetic to Jews, and the Jewish intelligentsia had traditionally been part of their circles. Among Jewish liberals were prominent jurists, writers, doctors, and wealthy merchants, as well as renowned Zionist leaders from Moscow, St. Petersburg, Kiev, Minsk, Warsaw, and Odessa.

But the sun of liberalism did not shine upon Russia for long. A bitter attack against the Kerensky liberals was instigated by the communists under the leadership of Nikolai Lenin[19] and Leon Trotsky.[20] Although neither Trotsky nor Lenin had been in Russia at the time of the Kerensky revolution, they quickly returned from abroad to take control. They conducted a noisy campaign among the soldiers and workers, exhorting them to overthrow the weak Kerensky government. The communist leaders promised the soldiers an end to the combat. To the workers they pledged control of the factories where they worked, and to the impoverished peasants, the land to be confiscated from the nobility.

Lenin and Trotsky won over not only the large numbers of soldiers, who had no desire to go to the front to fight the Germans, but also the workers who were starving and the peasants mired in poverty. Without its Western allies, the Kerensky government was unable to end the war, and thus could not deliver to the workers and peasants the promises of the communist leaders.

Although the communists took power in Moscow, they did not control the Empire as a whole, and in certain areas opposition to the communists surfaced. This resistance did not come from liberals, or from democratic groups, but from generals and gangs of hooligans.

A bloody civil war ensued in which much Jewish blood was shed. The bands fighting the communists accused the Jews of siding with the communist leaders in the Kremlin. The Jewish community was held responsible for the deeds of Leon Trotsky and other Jews who were then associated with the communists. Even Lenin was portrayed as a Jew by the anti-Semites. Pogroms were perpetrated in many cities, but especially in the Ukraine under Generals Denikin and Petlura,[21] who distributed stolen Jewish property among the peasants who supported them.

When the communist revolution began, many Jewish merchants, fearing they would be persecuted as class enemies, fled to areas beyond communist control. Several travelled as far as Siberia where they fell into the bloodied hands of other White Army bands led by generals Kolchak and Wrangel.[22] Thus, even those Jews who were fleeing communism were killed as supporters of the Reds, Lenin and Trotsky. The White Army also attacked the Jews in Byelorussia, and there, too, Jewish blood flowed like water.

In response to the pogroms, Jewish leaders in the United States and Canada attempted to intervene on behalf of their suffering co-religionists. However, there was no power on earth that could stop the pogroms. Although people suspected that the generals responsible were receiving aid from foreign sources ostensibly for fighting communism, the governments of Britain, France, and the United States denied any direct connection with the White Army generals. The pogroms ceased only after the Red Army had won the civil war, dispersed the anti-Semitic bands, and imposed order to the extent possible under the circumstances. When peace was restored, it became evident that the Jewish communities of southern Russia had paid a terrible price.

A fervent campaign was launched by the Jews of North America to aid the Jewish victims of the Russian civil war under the slogan "Bread for the living and shrouds for the dead". Canadian Jews played a significant part in all the major relief efforts initiated in the United States for this purpose, including a large-scale campaign to collect clothing.

Zionism in the First World War

Zionist Unity Shattered by World War I. The New Zionist Orientation
Conceived in Canada. Historic Conference in Montreal.

BEFORE THE OUTBREAK of World War I, the Jews of Germany were connected
to the Jews of Russia and other countries through the Zionist movement. In
Germany and Austria there were no compact Jewish communities such as
those in Russia, Poland, Lithuania, and Bessarabia. German and Austrian
Zionist leaders were mostly professionals—doctors, lawyers, professors, and
wealthy merchants. At Zionist conferences they would meet with Zionist
leaders from Eastern Europe, France, England, and other countries.

With the advent of World War I, the unity of the Jewish people was
shattered. Jewish soldiers from Russia, England, the United States, and Canada
were forced to fight against Jewish soldiers from Germany. At that time the
Germans were relatively free of anti-Semitism. In the German army there were
Jewish officers, whereas in the Russian army a Jew could not become an officer.

The World Zionist Organization became paralysed. Zionist leaders from
Berlin and Vienna could no longer meet with Zionist leaders from Vilna,
Odessa, or Warsaw, nor with Zionists from England, Canada, and the United
States. This precipitated a serious crisis for Zionism, especially since Eretz
Israel[23] (Palestine) was then under the rule of the Turks who were allies of
Germany.

The Zionist movement, however, did not cease to exist. Efforts on behalf
of Eretz Israel continued in England and North America, the United States
and Canada. Montreal became an important centre for Zionist activities. In
England Dr. Chaim Weizmann became the central figure in the Zionist
leadership. A famous chemist, he made a significant contribution to the British
war effort on the scientific front, and was very influential in British government
circles.[24]

Nahum Sokolow,[25] one of the greatest Jewish scholars,—a well-known
intellectual and journalist—settled in England where he became a dominant

personality among the Zionist leaders. He and Dr. Weizmann met with representatives of the British government to discuss the creation of a Jewish homeland in Palestine. These negotiations led directly to the Balfour Declaration in which England promised the Jewish people a national Jewish home in the "holy land".

When England was drawn into the war against Turkey, it was hoped that the British government could play an historic role in the realization of Zionism, that once Britain had wrested Palestine from the Turks, it could create a Jewish homeland. Because Canada had gone to war to aid the motherland, Canadian Zionists believed they could play a vital role in political Zionism. It seemed natural that Canada's influence in attaining the Zionist goal could be significant. Indeed, Zionist activity in Canada intensified during the First World War.

As early as 1915, Zionist activists in Montreal were convinced that Zionist policy must change, that instead of relying on Turkey, it was better to support England. To formulate this new position, the Canadian Zionist organization called a conference of Zionists as well as unaffiliated Jews. Its aim in uniting the Jews of Canada was twofold: first, to demonstrate their loyalty to both Canada and England, and secondly, to express the wish that England take Palestine from the Turks and give the Jewish people the possibility of building a national homeland there.

Because this historic conference[26] was of critical importance for the Zionist movement, the most distinguished leaders of American Zionism attended, among them Louis D. Brandeis[27] and Jacob de Haas.[28] The guest speaker, Dr. Shmaryahu Levin,[29] an outstanding figure among world Zionist leaders, enthusiastically endorsed, in Hebrew, the new Zionist orientation conceived in Canada.

An important guest at the conference was the honourable Arthur Meighen,[30] a member of the federal Cabinet. Addressing the conference in the name of the Government of Canada, he stated that once the Allies had won the war, the Jewish people would most certainly be treated fairly and justly.

In the spring of 1917, the British foreign minister, Lord Balfour, visited Canada. He also spent a few days in Washington with President Woodrow Wilson. Upon his arrival in Washington, Lord Balfour summoned Clarence de Sola,[31] president of the Canadian Zionist Organization, to discuss England's stance with regard to Zionism. Returning from Washington, De Sola was jubilant. Lord Balfour had informed him that England would soon make a public declaration to the Jewish people with regard to Palestine. Balfour had given De Sola a "preview" of the planned declaration.

The official Balfour Declaration was proclaimed in November of 1917. Of course, it was joyfully received by Zionists and Jews in general as a historic document. However, the tone of the declaration elicited a certain measure of disappointment among the younger, more dynamic Zionist activists. They recognized in this document certain political limitations which would restrict the possibility for the complete realization of Zionist aims. Among Montreal Zionists strong opposition arose to Clarence de Sola, in particular with regard to his position on political Zionism in light of the Balfour Declaration.

De Sola maintained that the Balfour Declaration had resolved all the problems of political Zionism, and that henceforth everything could be left to England. The opposition contended that it was only the starting point for political work. Younger Zionists were extremely disappointed by de Sola's attitude, accusing him of wanting to "liquidate" political Zionism. Among his opponents were Louis Fitch,[32] Michael Garber,[33] Benjamin Weiner,[34] and Bernard Jacobs,[35] now Dov Joseph, the justice minister of the State of Israel.

At the Zionist convention of 1919, held in Toronto, this issue sparked a dramatic debate. De Sola resigned from the leadership, and A. J. Freiman of Ottawa took his place as president of the Canadian Zionist Organization. With the Freimans a new chapter began in the history of Canadian Zionism. The Freimans were closer to the Jewish masses yet, at the same time, had strong connections in government circles in Ottawa, where they used their influence to further Jewish causes. The most illustrious personalities in the Zionist movement would often visit the Freimans in Ottawa to discuss crucial issues relating to the Land of Israel.

In addition, Mrs. Freiman played a decisive role in relief efforts. In 1920 she organized a large relief campaign on behalf of Jewish orphans in the Ukraine who had lost their parents in the pogroms of 1919. She convened a conference in Ottawa of Jewish leaders where it was decided to bring as many orphans as possible from the Ukraine. To promote this project, Mrs. Freiman travelled all over Canada. Jews everywhere responded enthusiastically, donating money and registering as "parents" to adopt the orphans upon their arrival.

A special emissary, H. Hershman,[36] was sent to the Ukraine to select 150 children orphaned by the pogroms and bring them to Antwerp. Mrs. Freiman sailed to Antwerp to meet the children and accompany them to Canada. This was one of the large-scale relief efforts carried out by Canadian Jews soon after World War I in which Lilly Freiman played a leading role.

However, Lilly Freiman was better known to Jews in Canada, as well as abroad, for her Zionist activities as president of the Canadian Hadassah Organization, which was always the largest organization for Jewish women in Canada. Mrs. Freiman dedicated herself, heart and soul, to Zionist activities. She played a pre-eminent role in every project undertaken on behalf of Eretz Israel in the 1920s. In addition to bringing the Hadassah movement to all parts of the country, she made her mark in the history of the Jews of Canada as one of its most distinguished leaders, both with regard to her Zionist activities as well as all her relief work for the benefit of the stricken Jewish communities across the ocean.

Zionist Conference, Ottawa, 1912
Canadian Jewish Congress National Archives

The End of World War I

Organizing the Canadian Jewish Congress. The Major Tasks of the Jewish
Communities. The Impact of the Balfour Declaration on Jewish Life.

THE AFTERMATH of the First World War presented serious problems for Jews
all over the world. They were faced with tremendous tasks requiring organization on a massive scale. The most pressing were the development of the
Land of Israel in conformity with the Balfour Declaration and immediate
assistance to the Jewish communities of Eastern Europe, ravaged by war and
pogroms.

Although the war was over, peace had not yet come to the majority of
Jews in Eastern Europe. In Russia the Bolshevik revolution had unleashed a
civil war which caused untold suffering to many Jewish communities. Anti-
Bolshevik groups perpetrated pogroms on the pretext that Jews were siding
with the communists. In the United States and Canada large sums of money
were raised to alleviate the suffering Jewish communities across the ocean.

Even before hostilities had ceased, a strong movement was underway to
organize the Jews of the United States and Canada to meet the great challenges
posed by the war. In both the United States and Canada there came a call for
the creation of a Congress in which Jews of every shade and stripe would be
represented.

In the beginning there was opposition from certain quarters, claiming
that a Jewish congress was unnecessary. The general Zionists feared that a
non-Zionist majority in the Congress would make it more difficult to carry
out large-scale Zionist projects which at the time were very urgent.

The general socialists considered a Jewish Congress to be inconsistent
with the spirit of internationalism. In that era socialists believed that socialism
and nationalism were incompatible. "Canadianized" English-speaking Jews
were convinced that a congress could be interpreted as "separatism", as the
creation of "a state within a state". However, the opposition weakened as the
more affluent Jews came to realize that the world was changing. Socialist parties

were making gains in England, France, Germany, and other countries.

The initiators of the Jewish Congress were mostly Poalei Zion[37] groups and socially conscious general Zionists who believed that through a broad organization like the Congress, non-Zionist groups could be persuaded to become active on behalf of Eretz Israel.

The first session of the Canadian Jewish Congress was held in March of 1919. It opened with a prayer by Rabbi Zvi Cohen[38] in the Monument National Theatre. Lyon Cohen[39] then welcomed the 210 delegates from all over Canada. Among the speakers at the first session were Rabbi Dr. H. Abramovitz,[40] Reuben Brainin,[41] Clarence de Sola,[42] Peter Berkovich,[43] and a guest from the United States, Dr. Chaim Zhitlovsky.[44]

During the three-day meeting of the Congress, most of the speeches were in Yiddish. A resolution was adopted to send a delegate to Paris who, together with delegates from other countries, would present Jewish demands at the Peace Conference at Versailles. The two main demands were a Jewish homeland in Palestine and guaranteed equal rights for Jews of all countries. Elected to the executive of the Congress were Lyon Cohen as president and H. M. Caiserman[45] as general secretary.

In the first few years after its inception the Congress generated a great deal of excitement, becoming the official address of Canadian Jewry. One of its first major achievements was to participate, together with Jews from other countries, in the large delegation to Versailles representing Jewish interests at the peace conference. This was not a simple matter. There was much debate over what demands should be made on behalf of the Jewish people. Everyone agreed that the peacemakers be asked to secure the immediate implementation of the Balfour Declaration and the security of Eretz Israel as a homeland for the Jewish people. But not all were in accord with the demand for Jewish cultural autonomy in the newly independent states of Eastern Europe—Poland, Lithuania and Latvia—which had previously been part of the Russian Empire.

At that time it looked as though the groundwork had been laid at Versailles for a new world order, ensuring that war would never be waged again and that all national minorities would be guaranteed the security to develop their cultures while enjoying full and equal rights in all spheres. President Woodrow Wilson, considered one of the most liberal of the American presidents, was the central figure at Versailles.

To Versailles came representatives of all the countries of Europe demanding guarantees that war would never break out again. In the governments of all these countries, socialists and liberals were in the majority. A few regions which had formerly been part of the Russian Empire, had broken away to form independent republics.

Apart from Russia, the Polish Republic had a large Jewish population whose prospects for a healthy Jewish existence seemed bright. Although for Soviet Jews the future was uncertain, and it seemed unlikely that under the communist regime there could be freedom for religious or Hebrew cultural activities, there was no doubt that in the socialist democracies, Jewish communities would enjoy complete spiritual and cultural freedom as well as equal civil rights in every sphere.

At Versailles the smaller new states of Eastern Europe made a commitment to respect minority rights. It was anticipated that the Soviet government would follow the rest of the world in establishing a society in which the Jewish minority would find its place. Since a large number of Russian Jews were expected to take up agricultural work, Jewish leaders in America, like the multimillionaire Julius Rosenwald,[46] established ties with the Soviet leaders for this express purpose. The Soviets allowed the leaders of the Agro-Joint[47] into Russia to help finance the establishment of Jewish farming colonies. For some time after the First World War the hope persisted that Russian Jews, having survived the terrible pogroms of the civil war period, would receive the assistance required to help them make the adjustment to Soviet reality.

A great deal was expected from the socialist governments of the new states of Poland and Lithuania where a large part of European Jewry remained concentrated. With every opportunity to develop a healthy and productive Jewish cultural life, a free and fully enfranchised Jewish society would flourish in keeping with the principles of human rights and freedoms formulated by President Wilson and proclaimed at Versailles.

Unfortunately, it turned out that President Wilson failed to implement his program for a new liberal world order. The Treaty of Versailles did not give national minorities the freedoms they had been promised. The Jewish minorities in Poland, Rumania, and Lithuania were oppressed by groups of ultranationalist and reactionary anti-Semites. Anti-Semitism in Poland became a serious concern as frightening reports of attacks on Polish Jews began to circulate. The policy of the government of the new Poland appeared designed to force the Polish Jews to leave the country.

Jewish communities in the United States and Canada vigorously protested against the Polish government. The Montreal city council adopted a resolution, brought forward by Leon W. Jacobs, K. C.—who in 1919 was an alderman—denouncing the persecution of Jews. At the same time S. W. Jacobs, K.C.[48] introduced a similar resolution in the federal Parliament. The plight of Polish Jewry continued to deteriorate throughout the entire period of the 1920s and 1930s.

Gitel Helfand and Samuel Solomon Glass with their children Moishe, Irvine Israel, Helen, and Esther. Slupia Nova, Poland, 1921.
A decade later they managed to leave Poland and settle in Toronto.

Economic and Cultural Prosperity

The Effect of Post-War Prosperity. Changes in the Garment Industry.
Cultural Growth. The Dramatic Turn of Events.

THE EARLY 1920S witnessed a strong economic revival in Canada. Jews found themselves involved in new branches of industry, commerce, and real estate.

Important changes occurred in the garment industry. Factories moved from the old unsanitary sweatshops into well-ventilated modern buildings where it was easier and more comfortable to work. Organized by powerful unions, workers laboured under collective agreements which obviated the need to strike as often as during the immigrant years prior to World War I.

The cultural level of the Jewish masses was also transformed. After the First World War Jewish culture and literature flourished. From Europe, especially Poland and Lithuania, came large numbers of Jewish intellectuals, among whom were famous Yiddish writers, poets, artists, and cultural enthusiasts. The influx of this intelligentsia greatly enriched the Yiddish press as well as Yiddish culture in general, in both the United States and Canada, and infused all community activities with new spirit.

A strong desire for higher education led to a considerable increase in the number of Jewish students in high schools and post-secondary schools. Many Jewish young people from the families of workers or small businessmen, determined to escape the clothing factories, found their way to colleges and universities. The economic prosperity created by the war gave working-class parents the opportunity to send their children to high school. The most able among them were soon admitted to university. The daughters of working-class parents trained as bookkeepers or stenographers to avoid the sweatshops. Thus began a profound transformation in Jewish life. Soon businessmen, merchants, shopkeepers, and professionals began to outnumber the factory workers.

The new wave of immigration also included more scholars, *maskilim*,[49] Zionists and Hebraists.[50] Experienced and qualified teachers arrived whose influence was keenly felt. As a result, the Jewish community acquired a new spiritual and cultural face.

The character of Jewish community work was fundamentally altered. Large-scale projects on behalf of Eretz Israel and overseas relief brought Jews together from all over Canada. National conferences or conventions, attended by representatives of various Canadian Jewish communities, often took place in Montreal or Toronto. The two major national organizations, the Canadian Jewish Congress and the Zionist movement, branched out across the country, from the Atlantic to the Pacific.

The economic and cultural growth of the Jewish community was vividly reflected in the large fund-raising campaigns conducted on behalf of Eretz Israel as well as in aid of the Jewish victims of war and pogroms in Europe.

During this time of cultural prosperity sizeable Jewish publishing companies were founded in New York, producing numerous Yiddish works of history, science, poetry, and fiction. Yiddish newspapers featured well-known journalists, literary critics, essayists and novelists who before coming to America, had been associated with the Yiddish press in Eastern Europe.

The post-war immigration brought to America many Jewish actors who had already achieved fame in Russia and Poland. The Yiddish theatre companies they founded often visited Montreal where they would perform in the Monument National or His Majesty's Theatres. They presented not only the best of the Yiddish repertoire but also plays from the world stage.

Performances in Montreal by actors belonging to the famous Vilna Yiddish Theatre Company, the *Vilna Troupe*[51] or the Habimah Theatre of Moscow[52] attracted huge audiences from among the intellectuals. It was a great event in theatre circles when a theatre company with Maurice Schwartz [53] would come to perform *The Dybbuk*[54], or H. Leivick's *Shmates*[55], or when Jacob Ben-Ami[56] starred in Peretz Hirschbein's *Grine Felder*[57]. Rudolph Schildkraut[58] was also among the great actors who used to appear on the Yiddish stage in Montreal.

Famous Jewish intellectuals and journalists would often come to deliver lectures on current Jewish or general problems or on philosophical subjects, always drawing large crowds. Discussions would follow the lectures with members of the audience asking questions which the lecturer would answer. Most of the Jewish topics at that time were related to Zionism. What basis the Land of Israel should be built upon was the subject of much controversy. At the beginning of the 1920s there were still ideological anti-Zionists. Occasionally the speaker was one of them. The Zionists would barrage him with questions and engage him in heated debate. Of course, when the speaker was a Zionist, the questions would come mostly from anti-Zionists. The latter, generally speaking, were socialists who believed that socialism and Zionism were incompatible. Ideological anti-Zionism, however, steadily waned.

Quite frequently speakers would lecture on the Bolshevik revolution in Russia. This was a delicate subject which led to sharp exchanges and even fist-fights. When the speaker was a leftist, he would describe the communist leaders of Russia as the authentic interpreters of Marxism and true bearers of the social revolution for all humanity. Such a speech would elicit angry shouts and protests from "right-wing" socialists, who would counter that the Bolshe-viks were subverting the social revolution by suppressing civil rights.

During a debate such as this, disputes would break out over whether or not Marxist and socialist ethics justified the dictatorship of the proletariat. Both sides would get very agitated. The sparring would end late at night. The next day, after the lecturer had already left town, members of the audience would continue to argue among themselves in the sweatshops or wherever they happened to meet.

Uptowners and Downtowners

Prosperity Creates a New Jewish Middle Class. New Philanthropic Institutions. *Landsmanshaftn* and Loan Societies.

IN THE FIRST YEARS after the Great War, the more affluent and established Jews known as "uptowners" lost their prominence in the community. Some "downtowners", former immigrants, benefiting from the post-war prosperity, had also become quite comfortable. Others became very wealthy.

Many of those who had worked their way to the top of the economic ladder moved to Westmount, becoming neighbours of the prosperous Jews who had already lived there for quite some time prior to the war. Others relocated to Outremont, also a fine residential district, which soon became a Jewish neighbourhood. New streets and attractive houses were hastily constructed, and in moved former downtowners who, having been successful in their businesses, had become more or less well-to-do.

The new homeowners, still attached to the traditions of Eastern Europe, did not want the uptowners to dominate the community's philanthropic and social institutions. They built large synagogues in Outremont—Adath Israel, Young Israel—and founded new Jewish institutions for charitable and social purposes.

In those years the difference between uptowners and downtowners increasingly diminished. Former downtowners became the owners of large homes, invested in real estate, and opened clothing factories in competition with the older established clothing firms. Large Jewish wholesale businesses selling dry goods and textiles came into existence. Jews also began to gain access to St. James Street and trade on the stock market.

Great changes occurred in the cultural sphere as well. All cultural activities were enhanced. The Jewish Public Library in particular grew substantially. Thanks to the newly emergent middle class, it became possible to raise larger sums for overseas relief and Zionist causes. Middle-class Jews became the leaders and activists in the large-scale efforts to rescue the beleaguered Jewish communities across the ocean. Although they now lived in comfortable homes, they had not forgotten the deprivation and poverty they had endured years ago in the old country.

During that same period, several *landsmanshaftn*[59] were founded to assist the suffering Jews in the cities and towns of the old country. The news from these places was very bleak. Everywhere Jews were being persecuted on a variety of pretexts. In Poland Jews were blamed for siding with the Bolsheviks of whom the Poles were terrified. The Polish government was led by nationalists who looked upon Jews as alien and superfluous. Nevertheless, Polish Jews fought hard for their rights. In the Polish *Sejm*[60] as well as the senate, there were courageous Jewish deputies who, on a daily basis, carried on the struggle against local anti-Semites. Jewish newspapers in New York and Montreal often carried articles about the brave speeches of Yizhak Gruenbaum[61] and other Jewish representatives. Their speeches, however, were of no avail. Political and economic anti-Semitism intensified. Poles would tell Jews to "go to Palestine!" Indeed, there were Jews who did leave Poland in those years for Palestine. Active Zionist youth organizations trained many young people to be *chalutzim* (pioneers) in Eretz Israel.

Polish Jews in Montreal and Toronto formed themselves into small *lands-manshaftn*[62] as well as into a large national organization called the Association of Polish Jews. This organization of immigrant Jews with strong ties to relatives and friends in the old country, and to its culture and way of life, played an important role in the Jewish community in Canada. The Association of Polish Jews was very active in the 1920s and 1930s, often sending delegates to Ottawa to protest against the anti-Semitic policies of the Polish government and to demand that Canada intercede on behalf of the Jews of Poland. The Association of Rumanian Jews was involved in similar activities since Rumania was also a centre of anti-Semitic activity in the 1920s and 1930s.

During this period downtowners also created loan syndicates for the purpose of providing loans to small and middle-sized businesses on a commercial basis, rather than on the basis of interest-free loans (*gmiles-khsodim*) from the Free Loan Association.[63] The Free Loan Association had begun to seem like a charity, whereas borrowing from a "Loan Society" meant "doing business". For some time these societies played a recognized role in the community. When a conference was convened to deal with an important community matter, the loan syndicates sent a good number of the delegates. Whenever an appeal for funds was made on behalf of a community institution in need, they would respond with sizeable contributions. However, in time they lost their usefulness, most of them were disbanded, and only a small number remained.

By the 1930s the barriers between downtowners and uptowners had almost completely disappeared. In every Jewish institution former downtowners became as influential as former uptowners. Today most of the leaders of these institutions and the biggest contributors to the large fundraising campaigns—for Israel, for overseas relief, and for local initiatives—are the sons and grandchildren of financially successful former immigrant Jews, who have become the equals of the grandchildren of the former uptowners.

Lafontaine Park, Montreal, 1933.

Organized Jewish Labour

Prosperity in the Clothing Industry. Political Influences Affecting the
Needle Trade Unions. Factional Struggles Between Left and Right.

AT THE BEGINNING of the 1920s the organized Jewish workers in the clothing
industry were an important part of the Jewish community. The unions in the
needle trades exerted a strong influence on all community matters and were
held in high regard.

During the war and the years immediately following, a strong industrial
revival took place in Canada bringing prosperity to many of the country's
citizens. The standard of living rose considerably. This economic upturn helped
to revitalize the clothing business as both men and women became better
dressed and more fashion-conscious. Consequently, working conditions in
the clothing trades improved considerably. This strengthened the unions in
the clothing industry.

Labour unions became increasingly involved in community and cultural
activities. The clothing workers' unions were preoccupied with raising money
for Jewish victims of war and pogroms in Europe. For a time it seemed as
though the needle trade unions were the strongest of all the labour unions in
Canada.

Somewhat later, still in the 1920s, the situation changed. Political disputes
within the needle trade unions left them weakened and even crippled. These
factional struggles between "left" and "right" afflicted many of the unions but
especially the "Jewish" unions of the needle trade workers.

Most of the leaders of the clothing workers' unions in those days were
dedicated social democrats with close ties to the socialist party and hostile to
all forms of dictatorship, including communist rule. On the opposite side were
those workers, already very vocal, who believed that the communist regime in
Moscow was a powerful ally in the fight against fascism and Nazi Germany.
Their opposition to fascism made them receptive to communist influences.
The communists then came out with slogans for a "united front" and sought

to bring the union leadership under communist control.

Originating in New York, the factional struggle soon spread all over Canada. It became so acrimonious that for a few years the larger unions, the International[64] and the Amalgamated,[65] lost all the gains they had made in the days when unity and solidarity had prevailed among their members.

The battle between left and right also had an impact on other parts of the Jewish community, especially in cultural and literary circles. The fear of fascism, and the hatred of the reactionary ideas which nurtured fascism, induced large numbers of writers and people engaged in cultural work to participate in the various forms of social action organized by the left.

For a long time the struggle between left and right had an adverse effect on Jewish life in the United States and Canada. Jewish cultural life was weakened. The greatest damage, however, was sustained by Jewish labour organizations, and in particular, the needle-trade unions.

The *Arbeiter Ring* (Workmen's Circle),[66] the largest fraternal organization of the Jewish masses and Jewish workers, which had played a decisive role in relief work for the victims of war and pogroms, was hit hard by this ideological wrangling. It actually split the organization in two[67] and poisoned relations among Jewish workers who had previously been strongly united.

In Montreal the feuding adversely affected both of the large labour unions, the International and the Amalgamated. In the Cloakmakers Union it reached the point where its members, sick and tired of the infighting, left en masse. For some time the activities of this union were halted. A schism occurred within the Amalgamated. The "leftists", together with other disaffected members, created their own Canadian Union of Clothing workers, which functioned for a short time. To obtain a collective agreement, this new union made significant concessions to the factory owners with regard to working conditions.

Both the tailors and the cloakmakers paid dearly for the factional infighting they had instigated. The situation did not improve until the beginning of the 1930s when the workers finally grew tired of quarrelling, and even more tired of the poor working conditions into which they had manoeuvred themselves. New attempts were made to revitalize the ailing unions, the International and the Amalgamated.

As conditions deteriorated in the needle trades, many workers left the sweatshops and tried their hand at other occupations. They opened small businesses, thus abandoning the ranks of the proletariat.

The leaders of the needle trade unions, including the millinery and fur unions, were mostly Jewish. They exerted a great deal of influence in general trade union circles, and also played a valuable part in certain Jewish community projects. They were especially involved in the *Histadrut* campaign[68] as well as in the activities of the Jewish Labor Committee.[69]

In recent years the *Arbeiter Ring* was given a new lease on life thanks to the immigration following World War II which included many people who had been affiliated ideologically with the labour movement in the old country. Among them were former *Bund*[70] activists from Poland who became very influential in the *Arbeiter Ring* and in the Jewish Labour Committee.

Tenth anniversary of the Jewish Labor Committee, November 1-3, 1946.
(From left to right) Bernard Shane, General Organizer I.L.G.W.U.; M. Lewis,
National Secretary of J.L.C.; A.R. Mosher, Ottawa, President Canadian
Congress of Labor; Michael Rubinstein, National Chairman J.L.C.; Jacob Pat,
New York Executive Secretary American J.L.C.; J. Silverstein, Winnipeg
delegate; K. Kaplansky, National Director, J.L.C.; Claude Jodoin,
Chairman of Trades and Labor Congress of Canada Standing
Committee on Racial Intolerance.

Jewish Education

The Sorry State of Jewish Education in the 1920s. The Dramatic Strike of the Talmud Torah Teachers. The Improvement during the 1930s.

JEWISH EDUCATION floundered during the 1920s. At the time, Canadian Jews were preoccupied with fundraising on behalf of the Jews of Europe and Eretz Israel, which they hoped would soon become a Jewish homeland in accordance with the terms of the Balfour Declaration.

Few people were concerned with Jewish education. For parents it was of little interest. During the immigration period Jewish education had been sorely neglected, and the majority of children received no Jewish schooling whatsoever. For religious Jews, their only concern was that their sons learn enough Hebrew to be able to say *kaddish*[71] "after 120 years". As for their daughters, they wanted them to be able to write Yiddish well enough to pen a letter to close friends in the old country when necessary. Therefore they tended to send their boys to the Talmud Torah[72] and their girls to the secular schools, where there was a positive attitude to both modern languages, Yiddish and Hebrew, as well as to secular Jewish literature.

Although in secular circles Jewish education was taken more seriously, opinions were divided as to whether to teach more Hebrew than Yiddish or more Yiddish than Hebrew. There was an ongoing and heated debate as to whether Yiddish would remain the language of the Jewish masses or whether Hebrew would prevail under the influence of a Jewish homeland in Palestine. Few people in those days could have foreseen that both languages would have to vie against English, which would infiltrate not only the social life of the Jewish community but also the synagogues. In the 1920s it looked as though secular Jewish culture in the Yiddish language would be the foundation of the social and cultural development of the Jewish community. This was the basic premise of secular Jewish education in the 1920s.

In the Talmud Torah the focus was on Jewish religious observance. Efforts were made to inspire in the students a sense of connection with, and enthusiasm for, the traditional synagogue. In the 1920s most of the schools were not as imposing and impressive as they are in the new suburbs where Jews live today. Lavish bar mitzvah celebrations were not yet in vogue. Students studied in classrooms housed in very modest premises.

At the beginning of the 1930s the situation improved. A campaign was launched to erect a modern building for the United Talmud Torahs, and in 1931 the new large Central Talmud Torah was inaugurated on St. Joseph boulevard, then the heart of the Jewish quarter. In this building students were taught in modern classrooms like those in the English schools.

The construction of the new building was a sign that traditional religious education was being taken much more seriously by the community. It was now possible to raise large amounts of money for this purpose. The costs of the new building were met by a campaign conducted at the height of the Depression following the stock market crash of 1929.

The new Talmud Torah building also served as a community centre. Large gatherings, convened for national or local Jewish causes, often took place there. Famous lecturers came to that building to speak on literary themes or subjects of general interest. During election campaigns Jewish candidates would hold their meetings in the new Talmud Torah. Previously, such meetings had taken place in Prince Arthur Hall. The atmosphere in the Talmud Torah was more Jewish, and even a political event had a more Jewish flavour there.

But even after the new building was completed grave problems remained. Not enough money could be raised to meet ongoing expenses, which were very modest in comparison with those of today. Teachers' salaries could not be paid on time. Weeks and months would go by without the teachers receiving any money. Representatives of the teachers frequently came to the offices of the *Keneder Adler* to complain about not receiving their salaries. Mr. H. Wolofsky,[73] the publisher of the *Keneder Adler,* would call the members of the Talmud Torah's board of directors into his office and confer with them on a course of action. Such consultations were not always successful. In fact, once, at the beginning of 1933, the teachers went on strike. They came to the *Keneder Adler* and declared that some of their colleagues were suffering from hunger to the extent that they simply did not have the strength to teach the children. This was one of the most moving strikes that I had the opportunity to witness. It was not a strike over higher salaries but simply a demand for unpaid wages. Each of the striking teachers was owed many months of pay.

The teachers were on strike for two months, exposing the lack of interest of the majority of Jews in Jewish education. All other community activities carried on as usual. Relief was collected for the suffering Jews of Europe and money was raised for Eretz Israel but the Talmud Torah remained closed. Only a small group of respected community members were concerned about the strike and endeavoured to settle it. The strike finally ended when the *Va'ad Ha'ir*[74] donated a sum of money to pay the teachers. Each teacher was given a portion of the debt owing to him.

To ensure that a strike such as this would never reoccur, the Board of the Talmud Torah was completely overhauled. New people were recruited, among them Lazarus Phillips, K.C.,[75] Mr. Abe Bronfman[76] and Mr. Ben Beutel,[77] the present chairman. With these people in charge the situation became very different. The teachers never again needed to strike for the non-payment of wages.

At the same time, the general state of education was ameliorated. The new leadership of the Talmud Torah brought beneficial changes not only to the financial situation of the teachers, but also to their teaching methods. It influenced for the better the attitude of the community toward Jewish educational institutions.

In later years, Jewish education was further enhanced when a new type of school was created in certain synagogues, the so-called congregational school. Schools like those in the Adath Israel, Young Israel, or Shaarei Zion, with their "day schools", became a vital component of the Jewish education system in Montreal. This development came about mainly because the younger generation of parents, who were Canadian-born, began to be more favourably disposed to Jewish education. Young English-speaking Jewish mothers proudly took their small children to learn *Yiddishkayt* and were prepared to pay the appropriate tuition fees. While parents in the past had not wanted to pay the required fees, the new generation of parents had more respect for the Jewish teachers and held them in as high regard as the teachers in the public schools.

When the Canadian Jewish Congress decided that the matter of overseas relief was no longer as pressing as in previous years it also got involved in educational matters. This had the effect of giving Jewish education greater priority in the Jewish community. The Jewish Congress created the *Fareynikter yiddisher lerer seminar* (United Jewish Teachers' Seminary) in order to satisfy the demand for new teachers more suitable for Canadian-born Jewish children. In recent years, the *Keren Hatarbut*[78] has also become involved in Jewish education under the direction of Rabbi Aaron Horowitz,[79] National Director of the Hebrew movement. Its primary task is to ensure that Hebrew schools have a complete educational curriculum. Hebrew schools in various parts of the country are under its supervision. Originally Rabbi Horowitz was in charge of Hebrew education for the entire region of Western Canada. In recent years, as director of the *Keren Hatarbut*, he is responsible for its activities on a national scale.

In September 1938, the cover of the Yiddish-language magazine for children, *Grinike Beymelekh* (Green Trees), published in Vilna, Lithuania, featured the rhythm band of Montreal's Peretz Shule on the occasion of the school's 25th anniversary. Standing behind her class is teacher Shulamis Borodensky (Yelin). *Courtesy of Prof. Dovid Katz*

Problems of Religious Jews

Frequent Disputes in the Community Regarding the Supervision of Kosher Meat.
A Quarrel that Ended in a Court Case. The *Va'ad Ha'ir*.

IN THE 1920S a marked revival began in religious Jewish circles. Observant Jews had been poorly organized during the immigrant era when the Jewish community in general was not yet well established. Secular Jewish groups, in the belief that Jewish nationalism and Jewish religious observance were distinct and ought to be separated, brought pressure to bear on religious Jews.

A large number of Jewish writers and journalists often manifested their hostility to religion and everything connected with the Jewish faith. They equated atheism and apostasy with radicalism and progress. Many people accepted the idea that to be a socialist meant to fight against religion and tradition.

Although socialists who espoused Jewish nationalism were not religious, they were more tolerant in their attitude to the synagogue. Many held the conviction that in Jewish life religion could be separated from Jewish nationalism.

During the immigrant era, religious Jews had been pessimistic. They were convinced that in this country there was neither a foundation nor a future for Jewish religious observance. Hence only two matters were of concern to them: first, that there should be kosher meat in their homes, and second, that their children should know a little Hebrew in order to be able to pray in the synagogue. As for other aspects of Jewish observance, they had lost all hope. They lived with a sense of foreboding that they would be the last generation of religious Jews on the American continent. However, after World War I, when more rabbis and scholars began to arrive from Europe and religious Jews became better organized, this gloomy outlook disappeared.

As the influence of the religious Jews increased, atheism declined as a force in Jewish social life. Publishing anti-religious articles fell out of fashion in radical and socialist newspapers. Socialists who were Jewish nationalists made peace with traditional religious texts, especially the prophets, whom they came to regard as social activists and Jewish intellectuals. The divide between the religious and non-religious was significantly narrowed.

During the war and the decade that followed, Canada enjoyed economic prosperity. This prosperity created a large class of successful businessmen among observant Jews. As the Jewish neighbourhood moved from the poorer part of the city into the more attractive uptown streets, spacious new synagogues were built which enhanced the prestige, status, and influence of the religious Jews in the community.

Yet serious problems remained for observant Jews, creating tension and friction. It proved extremely difficult to unify the religious community. There were frequent disputes among rabbis, *shokhtim* (ritual slaughterers), and storeowners over the supervision of kosher meat. From time to time these controversies had serious repercussions and deeply divided the community. Each side had its supporters. In those days kosher meat was a significant source of income for rabbis whose salaries paid by the synagogues were meagre and whose jobs were not secure.

In 1922 a *kehilla* ("community") was organized by a number of synagogues and organizations, to impose some order in the matter of *kashruth*. The organized *kehilla*, later expanded under the name of *Va'ad Ha'ir*, achieved very little during its first few years. It had opponents who refused to recognize its authority, and the conflicts continued. At times, well-respected members of the community would attempt to settle a dispute. Well-known rabbis were sometimes brought from the United States to mediate. On some occasions the issues had to be decided in a court of law. I happened to observe one of these cases in a Montreal courtroom. It is of interest to recount the following details without mentioning any names.

The *Va'ad Ha'ir* had accused a butcher of selling non-kosher meat as kosher. The charge was based on the law prohibiting false advertising. In this case the butcher had advertised that he was selling kosher meat despite the fact that the *Va'ad Ha'ir* had forbidden him to do so. Both parties had retained prominent lawyers. The defendant argued that his advertisement was completely true insofar as the meat he sold was kosher according to Jewish law.

The plaintiffs called an expert on *kashruth*, a respected rabbi who explained the notion of *kashruth* and its importance for the religious Jewish community. The defence also had an expert on *kashruth*, also a rabbi and a scholar, who declared that the defendant had complied with all the laws of *kashruth* under the supervision of competent *mashgikhim*.[80]

The plaintiffs claimed that the *Va'ad Ha'ir* spoke for the entire community, since the majority of the synagogues in the city belonged to it. The defence argued that the principle of "following the majority" (*akhrey rabim l'hatos*) was applicable in circumstances where there existed some doubt, but here there was no doubt because the defendant had obeyed the laws of *kashruth*.

The experts on both sides had come to the courtroom armed with books from which they cited the laws of *kashruth* and the rules pertaining to the authority of the organized Jewish community. Although the judge had a high regard for these books and the opinions of the Jewish commentators contained in them, he had no desire to get involved in this dramatic debate and asked the lawyers for both parties to do their utmost to persuade their clients to settle the dispute out of court.

The lawyers tried. "Neutral" community members also tried to have the quarrel resolved through mediation. Religious and other community leaders made every effort to organize the community in such a way as to eliminate this type of dispute. Although it took a long time, this process was finally successful. The *Va'ad Ha'ir* was broadened and fortified, bringing order into religious life and thereby raising the prestige of traditional Judaism in the community.

Labour Zionism

The Role of the Poalei Zion[81] and the Farband in the Organization of Jewish Life.
The Campaigns for Eretz Israel. Opposition to Zionism.
The Influence of the Histadrut.

THE POALEI ZION played an important role in the Jewish community in the 1920s. Then, as today, its members were active in all aspects of Jewish nationalism and culture. Their impact was felt both directly, through their own activities, and indirectly, because they influenced other groups to become involved in Jewish community projects. Within Poalei Zion circles were to be found a large part of the Jewish intelligentsia who were preoccupied with the issue of Jewish nationalism.

By the 1920s the Poalei Zion had widened its constituency to a considerable extent thanks to the existence of the Jewish National Workers' Alliance, the Farband. In addition to Poalei Zionists, non-partisan workers and Yiddish-speaking immigrants joined the Farband. The Farband had been organized in 1913 pursuant to a resolution adopted at a Poalei Zionist convention held in Montreal. The aim was to create a broader base for the Poalei Zion Party, which, at the outset, was quite small. The convention, which took place in 1910, recognized the fact that a mass movement was necessary to achieve its nationalist cultural agenda, first of all through Jewish education, and secondly by fostering a positive attitude on the part of the Jewish masses toward Eretz Israel.

The Poalei Zion and the Farband helped to create and maintain Jewish cultural institutions. Of course their first priority was to attract the Jewish masses, who in those days were mostly workers in the clothing industry. Many workers had been influenced by socialist idealists who had a negative attitude to Zionist causes even when those causes included socialism. Opponents of Zionism would argue that it was not practical to build a Jewish homeland in Palestine when Jews could be fighting for socialism in the countries where they lived. Zionism and nationalism, they claimed, were incompatible with Marxism and the class struggle. The Poalei Zion led an aggressive campaign to overcome the opposition of the socialists. Labour Zionists of today no longer have to engage in this type of debate. In fact, these arguments disappeared long ago and have been forgotten.

Most effective in defeating their opponents was the activity devised by the Poalei Zion and the Farband on behalf of the Histadrut in Palestine. These efforts were initiated in 1923, a few years after World War I. The Histadrut was founded because of the difficulties encountered by Jewish workers in obtaining employment with private colonists in Palestine. However small the remuneration paid to Jewish workers, Arabs were prepared to work for less.

At the beginning of the 1920s, the idealistic Jewish workers in Eretz Israel, the pioneering *chalutzim*, were forced into fierce competition for jobs. When they saw that their efforts were futile, a group of Poalei Zionists, including Ben Gurion, created the organization called the Histadrut to enable workers to become self-employed, without bosses. Initially the Histadrut operated on a small scale. Workers began producing grain on a cooperative basis and subsequently marketed the grain collectively. After that, they undertook the construction of roads linking one settlement to another. Eventually the Histadrut grew to become the largest organization in Israel today and the economic backbone of the Jewish state.

Prior to the launching of the Histadrut Campaign in the United States and Canada, the Poalei Zion had been establishing smaller funds for the worker *chalutzim* in Eretz Israel. At one point a "tool campaign" was organized, whereby tools were collected to send to Palestine. These campaigns were limited in scope, reaching only a small circle of people.

Once the Histadrut Campaign was inaugurated, the situation changed. Broader segments of the immigrant masses, especially workers, became involved. The Histadrut symbolized a labour organization which was socialist both in spirit and in deed. It won the respect of the needle trade unions, where the majority of the Jewish workers belonged.

The accomplishments of the Histadrut Campaign consisted not only in collecting extremely large sums of money for Eretz Israel, but also in bringing the ideal of Labour Zionism into circles which had previously been indifferent, cool, or even negative to activities on behalf of Eretz Israel.

In connection with the Histadrut Campaign, mass meetings were held in Prince Arthur Hall, or in other large halls, to which were invited trade union leaders like Joseph Schlossberg,[82] Secretary-treasurer of the Amalgamated, one of the most intelligent and idealistic of the trade union leaders, Abe Shiplacoff,[83] and Max Zaritsky,[84] president of the Millinery Union. The union leaders, who were also well-known socialists, used to make a forceful impression on the workers from the sweatshops and factories. Prominent Poalei Zion leaders came to address these mass meetings, people such as Yitzhak Ben-Zvi,[85] the president of Israel, who died not long ago, Zalman Shazar,[86] the present president of the State of Israel, Barukh Zuckerman,[87] and Golda Meyerson (Meir),[88] currently the foreign minister.

To the audience they would describe how the *chalutzim* in Eretz Israel were cleaving rocks for the construction of highways, draining swamps, and constructing *kibbutzim* on a cooperative basis, thereby ensuring the realization of a true socialist society in Eretz Israel.

In the 1920s and 1930s the Poalei Zionists played a major role in the Canadian Jewish Congress, both in the activities for overseas relief as well as in the battle against anti-Semitism. Representatives of the Poalei Zion and the Jewish National Workers' Farband were also active in the *Va'ad Ha'ir* to ensure that this community organization would support Jewish educational and cultural institutions.

In the 1930s the Poalei Zion movement had to concentrate principally on practical work for Eretz Israel. There were two main reasons for this. First, the Histadrut was constantly expanding its sphere of activity and was therefore in need of more assistance from the Poalei Zion groups in democratic countries. Secondly, Arab terrorism directed against the *yishuv*[89] was escalating. This made it necessary for all Zionist groups, including the Poalei Zion, to give priority to the situation in Palestine.

At the beginning of the 30s Zionists encountered serious difficulties, both internally and externally. Within the party there arose profound ideological and political divisions over the issue of whether to build the Land of Israel on a socialist or a capitalist basis. The clashes were mainly between the Poalei Zionists and the Revisionists.[90]

This internal struggle was also evident in Canada. Occasionally, one of the Revisionist leaders would attend a rally in Montreal or Toronto to speak out against bringing socialism to Eretz Israel. Among those who supported the Revisionists were the more traditional Eastern European Jews who were frightened by socialism. They saw any form of socialism as a deviation from Jewish nationalism.

Although the Revisionists did not have a large following, some of their leaders were able speakers who greatly impressed their listeners. Foremost among them was Vladimir Jabotinsky,[91] one of the bitterest opponents of socialist Zionism. In 1935 he visited Montreal where he addressed a large gathering in His Majesty's Theatre. Speaking before a full house, Jabotinsky, a brilliant orator, attacked the Histadrut and socialist Zionism in general. If socialism were established in Eretz Israel, the Jewish middle class and private enterprise would not settle there, and there would never be a Jewish state on both sides of the Jordan.

Because this meeting had been so well attended, and because Jabotinsky had received such an enthusiastic ovation, the Poalei Zion immediately announced that they would bring Zalman Shazar[92] to Montreal to respond to Jabotinsky.

Shazar, the present President of Israel, spoke before a large audience at the Mount Royal Hotel. He emphasized that it was the socialist orientation of the Histadrut which inspired the Jewish workers and *chalutzim* who were building Eretz Israel with such dedicated idealism, and that only through cooperative efforts would Eretz Israel be transformed into a flourishing and productive *yishuv*.

Many Jews who had heard Jabotinsky also listened to Shazar. For a long time there was much discussion as to who was right. The Poalei Zionists believe that history has proven Shazar right.

The external problems of Eretz Israel, as well as the struggle against Arab terrorists and the unfriendly mandate government, preoccupied the Labour Zionists in the United States and Canada. Very often Labour Zionists had to protest to the British Labour Party about the hostile attitude to Zionist aims manifested by the colonial minister, who was in fact a socialist (like Lord Passfield[93] and later Ernest Bevin[94]). In the 1930s the leaders of the Poalei Zion were very busy battling the leaders of the Labour Party over the inconsistency of their policy toward the socialist leaders of the Histadrut.

The Poalei Zion movement was constantly growing. New branches were created. The Farband became a large mass organization, and the Pioneer Women evolved into a network of Zionist women's branch organizations. As a result, the Actions Committee was formed to unite all the various groups within the Labour Zionist movement. The founder of the Actions Committee was Moshe Dickstein,[95] the first national president. Through the Actions Committee, the Labour Zionist movement became a powerful force in Jewish life in Canada. Isidore Bobrove, Q.C.[96] and Dr. Hurwich[97] of Toronto, were the national presidents. When Dr. Hurwich left to settle in Israel in the middle of his term of office, Leon Kronitz,[98] the current national president, was chosen to replace him.

The Actions Committee of the Labour Zionist Movement is affiliated with *Ehud Olami* in Jerusalem, which encompasses all the Labour Zionist organizations from a variety of countries, including the Mapai party[99] of the State of Israel.

Golda Meyerson (Meir), in Montreal, 1929, to address a mass rally organized by Poalei Zion.
Canadian Jewish Congress National Archives.

Zionism after the Balfour Declaration

The Impact of the Balfour Declaration on the Zionist Movement. Dramatic Meeting of the Zionist Leaders about the Ussishkin Emek Hefer Plan.

SOON AFTER the First World War the Zionist movement in Canada expanded substantially under the leadership of A.J. Freiman,[100] national president, and Mrs. Freiman,[101] president of Hadassah.

The Balfour Declaration had raised hopes for the slow but steady realization of Zionism. Optimists within the Zionist organization believed that the "restoration"[102] had finally arrived. Indeed in Canada, Zionists proceeded to create a Restoration Fund for the great and holy purpose of redeeming the land of Eretz Israel. The landowners in Palestine at the time, the Arab gentry, were prepared to sell their property for moderate prices.

Nevertheless, in those days work on behalf of Eretz Israel was not easy. Although, thanks to the Balfour Declaration, the prestige of Zionism had risen and the Zionist cause had been embraced by large sections of the Jewish population, a significant number of influential groups of well-to-do Jews remained indifferent and even negative to the aims and aspirations of Zionism.

Zionist leaders in both the United States and Canada tried to enlist non-Zionists in the cause of Eretz Israel. Some of the latter, persuaded to join a committee headed by Louis Marshall,[103] became known as the "non-Zionist Zionists". But a larger number of affluent American Jews, Marshall's colleagues in other Jewish philanthropic undertakings, remained cool to all endeavours linked to Palestine. When a Zionist convention or conference took place, most of the speakers in the 1920s spent their time berating wealthy Jews who refused to join or participate in the efforts on behalf of Eretz Israel. In Canada the situation was the same.

In 1927 Dr. Chaim Weizmann visited Montreal to launch the *Keren Hayesod* campaign.[104] He addressed a large crowd of Montreal Jews who responded warmly to his appeal. Dr. Weizmann was then the central figure in political Zionism, and his appearance in Montreal was a *yontef*, a day of celebration, for the Zionist section of the Jewish population. At a special luncheon in the Montefiore Club with a group of prominent philanthropists who had not yet joined the Zionists, Dr. Weizmann assured them that the Zionist ideal would surely be realized despite the many obstacles, including difficulties with the Arabs. He predicted that even if there were no independent Jewish homeland in our lifetime or that of our children, then certainly our grandchildren would live to see an independent Jewish state. Dr. Weizmann could not have foreseen at that time that a Jewish state would be created during his own lifetime, and that he would be its first president.

Around the same time Menahem Mendel Ussishkin[105] approached Canadian Zionists with a plan for Canadian Jews to contribute a large of sum money to the *Keren Kayemet*[106] to settle the Hefer Plain,[107] a vast swamp of 50,000 dunams, which would have to be drained. In the beginning, the leaders of the Canadian Zionist Organization were not enthusiastic about this project which seemed extremely impractical. Despite the controversy, it was difficult to refuse Ussishkin, who was the president of the *Keren Kayemet* and one of the most eminent leaders of the Zionist movement. This was in 1927.

As a reporter for the *Keneder Adler*, I attended a meeting of the Zionist executive which took place in the Chateau Laurier Hotel in Ottawa to discuss the issue. Mr. Freiman, the national president of the Zionist Organization, was so ill at the time that he was confined to a bed under the care of a nurse in an adjoining room.

The meeting began in the afternoon and continued until late at night. There were some very dramatic moments. Almost everyone present was against Ussishkin's proposal. Most were of the opinion that a large sum of money should not be gambled on a swamp when dry land was available for purchase. They were afraid that Ussishkin did not grasp the dangers involved in such an undertaking. One man who strongly supported Ussishkin's plan, however, was Hirsh Wolofsky, the publisher of the *Keneder Adler*. Late that night the Freimans made a decision. Throughout the debate Mrs. Freiman had been extremely distraught. On the one hand she agreed with those who argued that the people's money should not be invested in risky ventures. On the other hand, she agreed that in building a country risks had to be taken. She also appreciated Ussishkin's point of view, namely, that this was not really a gamble as long as there were Jewish workers in Eretz Israel willing to perform menial labour such as draining swamps.

After the executive had finally decided unanimously to approve the Ussishkin Emek Hefer project, the plan was brought before the 21ˢᵗ Zionist Convention in Winnipeg. The Zionist Organization assumed a large bank loan of $200,000 to launch this project. This was one of the great achievements of Canadian Jews on behalf of Eretz Israel. The Hefer Plain is today one of the most fertile areas in the State of Israel.

Thanks to this project the prestige of Zionism in Canada was strongly enhanced, and the Zionist movement in general became much more influential.

Kibbutz Kfar Menachem, 1937.
In the centre of the top row is Oda Stolman (later Ada Gilan) who left
Montreal after graduating from Baron Byng High School
to settle in Palestine.

Religious Zionism

Influence of Religious Zionism on the General Zionist Movement.
Mizrachi Then and Now. Bar Ilan University in the State of Israel.

THE MIZRACHI ORGANIZATION[108] in Canada has a long history. It was founded here at the same time as in Europe, at the dawn of the twentieth century. One of the founders of the Mizrachi movement was the rabbi of Lida, Isaac Jacob Reines,[109] known in his day throughout the Zionist world as a distinguished participant in Zionist congresses. He was the founder of a yeshiva, the Lida Yeshiva, and the author of a large number of scholarly religious books.

Rabbi Reines developed the idea, which was then quite new, that nationalism and faith were interconnected in Jewish life and could not be separated. He criticized modern Zionists who maintained that one could be a good and ardently nationalistic Jew even if one were not religious. At the same time he opposed the view that Jewishness was merely a matter of religion and had nothing to do with nationalism.

As I have already said, Rabbi Reines was one of the early founders of Mizrachi. During his lifetime, even before World War I, there were already Mizrachi groups in Canada.

I shall take this opportunity to mention that I had the pleasure of meeting three people here in Montreal who had been students at the Lida Yeshiva around the same time that I attended that institution. They are: Mordecai Mendelson, the principal of the Adath Israel School, Chaim Maisel, an active leader in Keren Hatarbut and vice-president of the Canadian Zionist Organization, and L. Yalofsky, a Hebrew teacher. They are all excellent Hebraists and learned in *khokhmes yisroel*, Jewish law and lore.

Among the great leaders of the Mizrachi was Rabbi Abraham Isaac Kook,[110] who for a time was the chief rabbi of Eretz Israel. He also headed a yeshiva in Jerusalem and was known throughout Jewish world as a *gaon*, a great scholar and intellectual. At the beginning of the 1920s Rabbi Kook paid a visit to Montreal accompanied by two other famous scholars, Rabbi Shapira, the

Kovno rabbi[111] and Rabbi Moshe Mordecai Epstein.[112] They toured North America with the aim of strengthening the foundations of traditional Jewish learning.

Rabbi Meir Berlin,[113] also one of the leaders of World Mizrachi, came from a family of great scholars in Lithuania. His father, Rabbi Naftoli Zvi Yehudah Berlin, was the founder of the Volozhin Yeshiva, one of the most renowned yeshivas in the Russian Empire.

Rabbi Judah Lieb Fishman,[114] another pillar in the Mizrachi leadership, was active in two major arenas: politics and culture. A prolific writer, he authored many learned books while at the same time playing an active role in Zionist political work. As a member of the Jewish agency, he was caught up in the bitter struggle against the mandate authorities and their anti-Zionist policies prior to the founding of the State of Israel.

In the early years, religious Jews were not very involved in the community. There were no urgent issues to spur them to action. Their main concern was that Zionist activity should not be separate from traditional Judaism. In particular, they fought against those who advocated the segregation of religion from nationalism or Zionism.

Rabbi Zvi Cohen,[115] chairman of the Montreal rabbinate, was one of the chief leaders of the Mizrachi movement in Canada in the 1920s and 1930s. Prominent rabbis from Toronto and Winnipeg were also in the Mizrachi leadership.

The major preoccupation of the leaders of Mizrachi was persuading synagogues to pursue the Zionist aim of building a national homeland in Eretz Israel. Many synagogue officials—presidents, administrators, and so on—were among the most active members of the Mizrachi organization and constituted the majority of the delegates to its conventions. To Mizrachi conventions came rabbis from various Canadian cities as well as prominent Mizrachi leaders from the United States. The guest of honour at such a convention would often be Rabbi Berlin, or Rabbi Zev Gold.[116] In those days religious Jews would respond with tremendous enthusiasm to their speeches, delivered in a familiar Old World Yiddish.

When it came to practical work for Eretz Israel or fundraising campaigns, the Mizrachi cooperated closely with the general Zionists. On certain projects, they worked together. At a convention of the general Zionists, Mizrachi activists were among the most illustrious delegates. The Mizrachi, as a group, differed from the general Zionists in that they were closer to the immigrant masses and spoke Yiddish. Among the journalists who were then very popular with the Mizrachi was Gedalia Bublik[117] of the *Yiddisher Tageblatt*,[118] who himself was also a Mizrachi activist.

The Mizrachi Organization grew significantly in the late 1930s, and again after World War II. The name of the Mizrachi leader, Rabbi Meir Berlin, was immortalized with the construction of Bar Ilan University in the State of Israel. The creation of this university, which is continuously expanding, is one of the greatest achievements of the Mizrachi movement in the State of Israel, and the Canadian Mizrachi can take much of the credit.

Just as the influence of traditional Judaism has become stronger in recent years, so too has that of Mizrachi, which is at present a vital part of the Zionist movement in Canada under the leadership of Joel Shterenthal,[119] national president, and Rabbi Tzemach Zambrowsky,[120] executive president.

Rabbi Kook toured North America with the aim of strengthening the foundations of traditional Jewish learning. This picture was taken during his Montreal visit, May 1924. Kook (centre) was accompanied on his trip by Rabbi Moshe Mordechai Epstein from the Sloboka yeshiva and Rabbi Shapira, Rabbi of Kovno. Canadian Jewish Congress president and community leader Lyon Cohen is in the back row, top far right. Next to him, top right, is Rabbi Herman Abramowitz from the Congregation Shaar Hashomayim. Lower left is Rabbi Zvi Hirsch Cohen. The man, third left in the back with top hat, may be Alderman Joseph Schubert.
Canadian Jewish Congress National Archives

Controversies in the Community

The Dispute over the Jewish School Question which Destroyed the Unity
of the Canadian Jewish Congress. The Election Campaign
which Divided the Community.

THE FIRST CANADIAN JEWISH CONGRESS was created to unite the Jews of
Canada for the purpose of meeting the great challenges facing the Jewish
people. This unity lasted for several years and then disintegrated.

The Congress unified the Jewish community in providing assistance to
Eretz Israel and the suffering Jewish communities on the other side of the
Atlantic. In the case of Eretz Israel, Jews were not in complete accord. Certain
groups remained indifferent to the idea of Zionism but they were not obstruc-
tionist. They stood aside and let the Zionists do their work. Although occasionally they would even make a friendly gesture by contributing to Zionist funds,
they did not join the ranks of the Zionists, nor did they want to identify with
the struggle for a Jewish homeland in Palestine.

However, all Jews were united in the work for overseas relief. Jews of every
religious and political persuasion did their utmost to support the relief efforts
on behalf of the European Jewish victims of the war and pogroms, even though
they did so through a variety of different organizations. When the Jewish school
question arose, it produced a serious schism within the community.[121] The re-
sulting dispute eroded the solidarity within Congress and impeded its activities,
leading to its virtual dissolution.

The school question divided the community into three groups. One group
took the position that the Jewish community should seize the opportunity to
create its own school system. In their own schools, Jews would be able to
introduce an intensive program of Jewish studies, and thereby educate a
generation conscious of its Jewish national identity. The opponents of a Jewish
school panel argued that Jews did not have the resources to run their own
school system. A second argument was that children educated in Jewish schools
would encounter difficulties integrating into Canadian society. Their English

would not be perfect, which would be an impediment in their future careers.

At first it appeared that this dispute, already very divisive, was only over technicalities. But it soon became evident that this was a thoroughly ideological quarrel over the principles governing the various approaches to Jewish nationalism and Jewish goals for the future.

The lines were drawn between two distinct ideologies. On one side were committed nationalists, who saw no contradiction between Jewish nationalism and Canadian citizenship. On the other side were those who believed that separate Jewish schools meant creating a Jewish ghetto within Canadian society. They called this "national separatism" and considered it contrary to the Canadian way of life.

This dispute generated much passion and bitterness. Numerous rallies and conferences were held in Prince Arthur Hall, then the primary venue for Jewish political gatherings (and also for weddings). The climax came during a provincial election campaign in the St. Louis Ward, which was then completely populated by Jews.

During the campaign, the proponents of separate Jewish schools supported the candidature of Louis Fitch,[122] who ran against Peter Bercovitch.[123] The latter was a prominent figure in the fight against "separatism". Bercovitch was a mainstay of the Liberal party under Premier Taschereau,[124] and the first Jew to be elected by immigrant Jews to the Quebec Legislature. His stand against separate Jewish schools antagonized nationalist groups who decided to oppose him on that issue.

Peter Bercovitch was one of the most able of the lawyers who actively participated in Jewish community work. He was a courageous fighter against anti-Semitism and in the forefront in the work for overseas relief. He was also the lawyer for the needle trade unions and therefore very popular among the workers and the immigrant masses.

Louis Fitch, known as an intellectual as well as a Jewish scholar, played a central role in the Zionist movement. Politically, he was affiliated with the Conservatives. The meetings on behalf of Fitch appeared to be more cultural than political in nature. The speakers were better known as cultural activists and nationalistic Jews who highlighted the importance of creating on the North American continent a school system administered exclusively by the Jewish community. Among the speakers at the Fitch meetings were Rabbi Cohen[125] and Reuben Brainin[126], who under no other circumstances would ever have become involved in political struggles. But they believed that they had to make an exception for an issue as important as separate Jewish schools. In their speeches they sharply attacked the trend toward assimilation. They claimed that Jews educated in Jewish culture and traditional learning would be better citizens of Canada than Jews who knew little or nothing about Jewishness. In the Bercovitch meetings speakers argued that it was an illusion to believe that Jews could run a separate Jewish school system in a city where Jews were a small minority.

In Christian circles there was no opposition to special Jewish schools. The courts recognized that Jews were entitled to their own school system. Premier Taschereau even introduced a bill into the Legislature aimed at allowing Jews to create their own Jewish school board, if they so wished.[127]

The election campaign ended in a victory for Bercovitch. However, the supporters of a separate school panel were gratified that in principle—in the opinion of the court—they had won. In time, the conflict over the school question subsided.

When he was elected in 1918, Peter Bercovitch became the first Jew to sit in Quebec's provincial legislature.
The Jew in Canada (Jewish Publications Ltd.), 1926.

The Crash of 1929

The Sudden Transition from Prosperity to Depression.
Former Stock Market Millionaires who Became Paupers.
How the Situation "Normalized".

IN THE 1920S, while Europe was still recovering from the dreadful wounds inflicted by the First World War, America was blessed with prosperity. People were earning a great deal of money and "living it up". It was the era of jazz and musical comedies. While great stars were born in Hollywood, the number of wealthy and well-to-do Americans continued to multiply.

Not everyone, of course, was prosperous. There were many poor people, especially among the workers. But the poor were convinced that their poverty was not permanent, that sooner or later their luck would change and they would find themselves drawn into the general prosperity which had brought happiness and freedom to so many.

One of the most direct roads to riches was the stock market. Wall Street opened its doors to everyone. Everyone was welcome to buy stocks and make money effortlessly. All types of people, rich and poor, took the road to the stock market. A wealthy man would invest a great deal, and a worker, the few hundred dollars he had saved for a rainy day. Overnight the stocks shot up in value and profits grew. Then up again, continuously climbing.

Businessmen spent more time in the offices of their stockbrokers than in their own businesses. Others went even further: they liquidated their businesses, sold their stores or sweatshops, and with the proceeds bought more stocks, which turned a quicker profit—at least on paper—than their former businesses. It reached the point where the price of each stock was twenty or thirty times higher than its actual value. A crash was inevitable.

The stock market burst like a bubble. Many people saw their fortunes vanish overnight. The crash of the stock market led to business failures on a massive scale. In the United States, banks and finance companies were forced into bankruptcy. Although in Canada the chartered banks were protected by government regulation, even here few people could escape the financial crisis which affected all sectors of the population. As factories closed and workers lost their jobs, the Jewish industries—clothing and textile—were among the hardest hit.

The usual charitable institutions lacked sufficient resources to provide assistance to all those in need. Former donors became as poor as the recipients of their charity. A businessman who owned a car had to worry about having enough money to buy a few gallons of gasoline.

Unemployment became a very serious problem. Many people roamed the streets in search of work which was impossible to find. When the unemployed marched to City Hall to demand bread and butter, the city administration had to scramble to provide as much relief as possible under the circumstances.

The following facts are sufficient to show how widespread poverty was in the Jewish community. The *Keneder Adler* appealed to those who had managed to escape the crisis to contribute to a fund on behalf of the victims of the Depression. From this fund, support would be given not to the poor but to the newly impoverished, those who only yesterday had been the owners of businesses and property. The money was to be handed to them in the offices of the *Keneder Adler* by a few prominent citizens in charge of the fund. Most of the contributions were brought directly to the offices of the *Keneder Adler*. As a staff writer for the newspaper, I used to help this committee in its effort to ensure that the distribution was orderly and discreet. The recipients were not to meet one another. This was to be a *masan beseyser*, a secret donation.

But this was not all. There was talk that people were going hungry in the Jewish street. An initiative was launched to open a people's kitchen, with the participation of activists from the Poalei Zion, the Farband, and the *Arbeiter Ring* (The Workmen's Circle).[128] H. Hershman[129] was in charge of the soup kitchen which existed for several years until the situation returned to normal.

In the United States, President Roosevelt organized the New Deal to save the sick economy from a complete breakdown. There the crisis was even more acute than in Canada. The failure of the large banks had forced many large, well-established businesses into bankruptcy. Roosevelt created a Brain Trust of eminent economists to rescue the financial structure of America.

When the situation stabilized, it was because preparations for war were again underway. Once more the political situation in Europe became chaotic. Hitler had destroyed the Weimar Republic and was arming his country on a massive scale. The Allies lost their control over the Germans and the Treaty of Versailles was completely shattered. In Italy, Mussolini and his fascist followers in their black shirts were in charge, while in Germany the brown-shirted Nazis went on a rampage. With Hitler threatening to declare war on the entire world to overthrow the communists and the Elders of Zion, no one knew whether he planned to attack the communists in the east or the democracies in the west.

During the Depression governments had spent large amounts of money on public works such as highways and other communal undertakings to create jobs for the unemployed. Then they turned their attention to the munitions industry, and this gradually dispelled the economic crisis.

The First Warning from Germany

Hitler Launches His Campaign against Jews, the Treaty of Versailles
and the Weimar Constitution. His Alliance with Ludendorff.
The Unsuccessful Nazi Putsch.

WHEN PEOPLE HERE first heard about Hitler at the very beginning of the 1920s, they considered him an idiot and not to be taken too seriously. But very soon, after seeing his name appearing more frequently in the news, his rallies attracting more attention, and former officers and soldiers among his followers, Canadian Jews became alarmed at the anti-Semitic agitation he was fomenting.

Adolph Hitler began his activities in Munich, Bavaria. Tension and unrest had been generated by the Treaty of Versailles, which had exacted a heavy price from the conquered Germans. Although Germans everywhere protested and rebelled against the steep payments imposed on them, in Bavaria these protests were noisier than anywhere else. The provincial government of Bavaria had in fact revolted against the central government in Berlin led by Fritz Ebert,[130] president, and Phillip Scheidemann,[131] chancellor, both Social Democrats.

In Versailles, the leaders of the Allied countries had shown no pity for the defeated Germans. They refused to deal with the Kaiser as well as the militaristic Junkers. The Kaiser abdicated and fled to Holland. The generals, Ludendorff,[132] Hindenburg[133] and the others, were allowed to remain in the country, but not in government. The Socialists took over the leadership of the state and drafted a liberal and democratic constitution, which became known as the Weimar Constitution.

The Germans were granted many liberal and democratic freedoms to which they had not been accustomed under the Kaiser. They shed their Junker militarism. While perhaps this would not have bothered them, they also lost their economic stability. The Allies took control of their heavy industry and closed down the giant munitions factories. Germany became a land of poverty and need. Large numbers of people, including many former soldiers and officers, found themselves out of work.

The Germans, extremely resentful, became receptive to agitators who advocated rebellion against the Allies and non-compliance with the Treaty of Versailles. Large groups of communists formed, inciting the workers to strike in revolt. Frequent clashes erupted between workers who sided with the communists and those who supported the socialists.

Then appeared Adolph Hitler, creator of a new and tragic epoch in the history of the world. He began by addressing the impoverished and desperate people in the street, the unemployed, disillusioned, and disaffected Germans. His speeches drew large crowds.

He attacked the communists and the socialists for advocating a philosophy created by a Jew, Karl Marx. Germany, he cried, is being oppressed by Russia on one side, and France and England on the other. Russia is under the leadership of Leon Trotsky, a Jew, while France and England are controlled by the Rothschilds, also Jews. The Jews, he claimed, are responsible for German suffering. German gold has fallen into Jewish hands, to Jewish bankers in Paris, in London, and on Wall Street.

Hitler began to attract the attention of the military and financial elites. He was seen as a force they could enlist against the communists they feared, the Treaty of Versailles they despised, and the democratic Weimar Constitution which was not at all to their liking. Hitler thus acquired important friends and supporters, among them the former chief of the German army, General Ludendorff.

In the beginning, as I have already mentioned, Hitler was not taken seriously. He was thought to be quite harmless. However, it soon became apparent that his influence was spreading, and that he was receiving both overt and covert financial support from powerful factions hostile to the Weimar Republic. Fear arose that what had taken place in Rome in 1922, when Benito Mussolini, a former editor of a socialist journal, marched into the Italian capital and imposed a fascist dictatorship, could repeat itself in Germany.

Many German Jews became nervous as they began to sense that they were in danger. Some of these frightened Jews started leaving the country in search of new homes. Around the same time, many assimilated German Jewish families reclaimed their Jewish identity and even became Zionists. Thus began the emigration of German Jews to Palestine. The impact of Hitlerism extended to other countries as well, causing assimilated Jews to return to their roots and embrace Jewish nationalism.

Of course Nazism also had a profound psychological effect on Jewish youth and the intelligentsia. Many Jewish intellectuals actively participated in movements to combat fascism and Hitlerism. Their main objective was to unite all liberal and democratic groups in the struggle against fascist influences. They believed that Nazi fascism was extremely dangerous for Jewish people everywhere, including the free democracies.

The rise of Hitler injected more urgency into Zionist efforts on behalf of Eretz Israel. There was a growing feeling that Jews were not safe, even in safe countries. No Jew could fathom how such barbaric anti-Semitism could exist in a country which had been the centre of European civilization. If this could happen in Germany, what could prevent it from happening in other civilized countries?

Not long before, when World War I ended, many Jews in a number of countries harboured the illusion that Europe would rid itself completely of anti-Semitism, that socialists would lead the governments of most European countries, and that Jews would enjoy freedom and civil rights. Socialist parties were on the ascendancy, not only in the defeated nations, Germany and Austria, but also in France, England, and in the Scandinavian countries. As for the Russian Jews, there was certainly nothing to worry about. Too many Jewish names were then in the Soviet leadership. In the Soviet Union, Jews would soon forget the taste of *goles*, exile.

Those Jews who were convinced of a democratic and socialist future for Europe, were cool to Zionist aspirations. They believed that the word *goles* was no longer realistic in Jewish life. This illusion was shattered when Mussolini seized power in Italy and Hitler appeared in Germany. Although Mussolini was not, in fact, an anti-Semite, he destroyed the hope that Europe was advancing toward democracy and socialism. On the other hand, there were Jews who thought that Hitlerism would not last long, that Hitler's party, the National Socialists, would soon disband.

In 1923, Hitler with a group of Nazis attempted a putsch against the provincial government of Bavaria. It quickly ended in failure. Hitler was arrested, and along with ten other Nazi leaders, among them the former general Ludendorff, brought to trial. While Ludendorff was acquitted, Hitler was found guilty and sentenced to five years in prison, which was considered a very light punishment. Evidently the judges were sympathetic to him. He stayed behind bars for only eight or nine months, after which he was let out on parole.

At the time of Hitler's release, the Nazi party was not very powerful. The economic situation in Germany had improved thanks to certain financial concessions which the Allies, especially America, had made to the Germans concerning their contribution payments.

With the Nazis in decline and Hitler no longer agitating for the overthrow of the Weimar Republic by force, many German Jews believed that the Nazi danger had passed and that Hitler no longer posed a threat. No one could know that within a few years the National Socialist Party would be ruling Germany.

The Rise of Adolph Hitler

The Economic Collapse in Germany after the Financial Crash of 1929.
How the Nazis Came to Power. The Disastrous Impact
on the Jewish Community.

THE ADVERSE EFFECTS of the Wall Street crash of 1929 were evident in many
of the European countries, especially those with close economic ties to the
United States. The collapse of the stock market brought ruin to many businesses
and financial institutions in England, France, and Germany. In Germany, it
provoked a serious economic crisis and political unrest. As a consequence,
Hitler resumed his activities, and his National Socialist Party became the largest
party in the Reichstag and then the ruling power in the country.

The great crash of 1929 meant a resumption of tragic news from Germany
about Nazi misdeeds which grew more aggressive and violent from day to
day. The Jewish communities of the United States and Canada were already
aware that the Jews of Germany and the rest of Europe were in danger.

To understand the return of Hitler one must go back a few years to Hitler's
arrest after his unsuccessful putsch in Munich. Although Hitler was in jail for
less than a year, upon his release Germany had already become more peaceful,
and the effects of the economic depression had decreased. In 1925 President
Ebert[134] died and was replaced by General Hindenburg.[135] Ebert had symbolized
the socialist society of the future, while Hindenburg signalled a return to militarism.

There was also a new chancellor, Gustav Stresemann.[136] Under Stresemann
the economic situation had begun to improve. Inflation had been contained
thanks to the Dawes Plan and the Young Plan,[137] pursuant to which tremendous
sums of money began to flow to Germany from America. In Washington and
London it was decided to save the German economy for two reasons: first, to
protect the Weimar Constitution from the Nazis and the communists, and
secondly, to enable the Germans to make their contribution payments as
required by the Treaty of Versailles.

The political situation also improved in 1925 because of the so-called Locarno Treaty which guaranteed German borders, providing, of course, that Germany complied with the terms of the Treaty of Versailles. While the economic and political conditions had stabilized, Hitler's followers could not make much noise. As long as the Germans were not hungry they paid little attention to the Nazis.

Under Stresemann Germany was admitted into the League of Nations and life became more or less "normal". Very few German Jews feared the Nazis. Jews were then very rooted in Germany and integrated into all branches of German life, including commerce, science, literature, and art. The largest German newspapers had Jewish publishers, Jewish editors, and first-rate Jewish journalists. These Jews never imagined that they would soon be dismissed from the established positions they had inherited from their parents and grandparents. They considered themselves Germans and had almost forgotten their Jewishness. Without being reminded by the Nazis, they would have given it little thought.

The effects of the stock market crash soon reached Germany. America began to withdraw its gold from German banks, large businesses became paralysed, and factories were shut down. Again Germany found itself with an army of unemployed workers, businessmen, and professionals.

Then Hitler reappeared with his oratorical demagogy. Once again people flocked to him in droves and joined the Nazis. Hitler shouted that Jewish bankers from Wall Street, London, and Paris were responsible for the economic crisis in Germany. He called upon the Germans to fight against the Treaty of Versailles created by the Jewish people, the true enemy of Germany.

The Nazis were extremely successful, and Hitler's book *Mein Kampf* became very popular. Germans read it avidly and it was translated into many languages. As Hitler broadened his political activities, German youth rushed to join the Nazi storm troopers parading in their brown shirts.

Many German workers were communists who had also become politically active as a result of the grave economic crisis which had left six million Germans unemployed. In Germany's industrial centres bloody street fights broke out on a daily basis between Nazis and communists.

In 1929 Heinrich Brüning[138] became the chancellor of Germany. To rescue Germany from Nazi rule he organized a movement to bring the Kaiser's family back to Berlin. He preferred the prospect of Germany ruled by a Kaiser to government by a Nazi dictator. His efforts failed.

When the Nazis won a large number of seats in the Reichstag in the elections of 1930, it became clear that they would most certainly come to power. Thereafter German Jews became truly frightened. Between 1930 and the autumn of 1933, when the Nazis took over the government of Germany and Hitler became chancellor, many Jews left the country. A large number settled in Eretz Israel and have become prominent citizens of the *yishuv*. With their intelligence and talent, they have made valuable contributions to the development of the present-day State of Israel.

Militant Anti-Semitism

The Rise of Arcand's Anti-Jewish Movement. The Struggle
against the Liberals over the Jewish School Question
during a Stormy Campaign against Jews.

IN THE 1930s a militant anti-Semitic movement emerged in the Province of
Quebec, especially in Montreal, led by Adrien Arcand,[139] whom we called "the
little Hitler of Quebec". Although there were other vociferous anti-Semites,
Arcand was the movement's central figure, its ideologue, initiator, and
organizer. He was the editor of a few slick and clever anti-Semitic newspapers,
which he published in close collaboration with Joseph Ménard, the owner of
a Montreal printing shop.

Two other anti-Semitic leaders who gained notoriety during that period
were Salluste Lavery, a second-rate lawyer, active mainly on the "political front",
and Dr. Lambert, a dentist and publisher of the book *La clef du mystère* ("The
Key to the Mystery"), a collection of anti-Semitic materials from various eras,
including the infamous *Protocols of the Elders of Zion*.[140] This book was widely
distributed in the Province of Quebec.

Arcand began his anti-Semitic activities in the 1920s with a series of articles
denouncing Premier Taschereau for introducing a bill in the Quebec legislature
granting Jews the right to their own school panel in the Province of Quebec.
Arcand then launched a campaign against the Liberal government in Quebec.
Taschereau's position with regard to the Jewish school question had presented
Arcand with an opportunity to attack the Liberal party on the grounds that
Taschereau had sold out to the Jewish community and betrayed the interests
of the Christian population, especially the Catholics.

The campaign against Taschereau over the Jewish school question
resonated strongly in certain French Canadian circles. Arcand's little newspaper
acquired a wide reputation and readership. Arcand also received the support
of political organizations interested in undermining the position of the Liberal
party in Quebec.

When he saw that his anti-Semitic merchandise was selling well, Arcand started another weekly paper, and intensified the campaign against both the Liberals and the Jewish community. At the same time, he organized a movement based on fascist and Nazi ideology. Its chief slogan proclaimed that all Jews were communists and most communists were Jews.

At the beginning of the 1930s, Arcand further expanded his anti-Semitic movement. He allied himself with foreign pro-Hitler organizations and became the spokesman of Goebbels and Streicher[141] in Quebec. In his periodicals, he reprinted articles from *Der Stürmer*,[142] and, of course, the *Protocols of the Elders of Zion*.

The success of Arcand and Ménard encouraged others to embrace anti-Semitism. A number of anti-Jewish groups were formed under various names. Some were interested mainly in the economic struggle against Jewish merchants and shopkeepers, and began to agitate for a boycott of stores run by Jews. Many Jewish shop owners in smaller cities and towns were adversely affected by this campaign.

As I have already mentioned, Salluste Lavery worked on the political front. During an election campaign he would run for office on an anti-Semitic program. In the municipal elections of 1934 he was one of the mayoral candidates. For the first time in the history of Montreal's municipal elections there was a candidate with no platform other than anti-Jewish slogans.

Lavery conducted a stormy campaign. At his rallies, anti-Semitic speakers would inflame the crowd with vicious speeches against Jews. He justified the persecution of Jews in Germany, and called for the same to be done in Canada. Although Lavery lost the election, he had nevertheless attracted a large number of votes, which of course caused great consternation in the Jewish community.

Canadian Jewish Congress National Archives.

The Campaign against the German Jews

Duplessis Launches a Campaign against German Jewish Immigration to Canada.
His Sensational Claim Regarding 100,000 Jewish Refugees. Dramatic Debate
in the Montreal City Hall about Jewish Victims of Nazism.

THE ANTI-SEMITISM of the early 1930s began to infiltrate the upper echelons
of political power. From time to time anti-Semitic slogans were heard in the
Quebec Legislature.

One day, Maurice Duplessis,[143] leader of the Union Nationale and long-
time Premier of Quebec, made an announcement, which was, in fact, a dangerous incitement against Jews. He disclosed that large numbers of German Jews
fleeing Hitler's regime were on their way to Canada, and, as a result, French
Quebecers were in grave danger. Duplessis claimed to have received this
information from reliable sources. No fewer than 100,000 Jewish refugees from
Germany were to be settled in the Province of Quebec on farms purchased
with money from world Jewry.

Mr. Duplessis' announcement caused a sensation. The English- and
French-language newspapers featured it as international news of the utmost
importance. Duplessis informed the Legislature that he was extremely
concerned about the fate of the 100,000 Quebec farmers who would lose their
farms to German Jews. He exhorted French Quebecers to demand that the
federal government in Ottawa shut the gates of the country to Jews forced to
flee Germany.

Mr. Duplessis's revelation reverberated throughout the cities and towns
of the province. Indeed, a strong campaign was soon organized to encourage
French Quebecers to demonstrate their opposition to allowing Jewish victims
of Nazi brutality into Canada. In Ottawa, the federal government made it
clear that it had no intention of opening Canada's doors to a massive influx of
German Jews.

In the city halls of many of Quebec's towns and villages, motions were
adopted demanding that the victims of Hitler not be allowed into Canada.

These motions sounded just like Nazi propaganda, referring to German Jews as antichrists and promoters of communism and atheism. The resolutions were often introduced by speakers who spewed fire and brimstone against Jews and justified their persecution at the hands of the Nazis. According to those speeches, the Jews in Germany were probably receiving the punishment they deserved.

A similar motion was tabled in the Montreal City Hall, sparking a very dramatic debate. This was in September of 1933. An entire session was devoted to the "Jewish Question". The resolution had been introduced by Alderman Auger,[144] already known as a bitter anti-Semite and member of Arcand's National Christian Social Party. Another notorious enemy of the Jewish people was Alderman Quintal.[145]

Many people attended this session, knowing in advance that a debate on anti-Semitism was about to take place. Alderman Auger opened the debate with a speech in which he demanded an acknowledgment that the leaders of the German state deserved the gratitude of all Christian people for persecuting the German Jews who were communist agents with anti-Christian objectives. The German Jews, he shouted, were conspiring with the rulers in Moscow to destroy Christian civilization everywhere, including here in Quebec.

Alderman Quintal spoke in the same vein. Other French Canadians expressed regret that German Jews were being persecuted, but allowing them into Canada? No. The federal government must be asked to bar further immigration.

Only three aldermen, all Jews, namely Joseph Schubert,[146] a socialist, Max Seigler,[147] and Berl Schwartz,[148] spoke in defence of the German Jews. Each of the three Jewish aldermen eloquently condemned the hypocrisy and demagogy of the anti-Semitic speakers. Special attention was focused on Joseph Schubert because he spoke not only as a Jew, but also as a socialist with close ties to the trade union movement. He said that the Nazis in Germany were bitter enemies of all civilized peoples, and that organized labour everywhere, including the Province of Quebec, was determined to fight against Nazi and fascist countries and all those who directly or indirectly supported them.

Alderman Seigler termed it vile and hypocritical to attack German Jews in the name of Christianity. All responsible Christian leaders in the democratic countries were condemning the Hitler government in Germany as barbaric and evil. Alderman Schwartz expressed his indignation that in a city like Montreal, with its cosmopolitan population, anti-Semitic speeches reminiscent of the Middle Ages could be delivered in the City Hall. Montreal was perhaps the only major city on the continent where such scenes of anti-Semitic demagogy and hypocrisy were tolerated.

Enraged, Alderman Auger jumped from his seat, shouting that Alderman Schwartz had insulted him. Later he approached the press table to tell the French reporters that he would not remain silent. He would get even with the Jewish aldermen, and would certainly sue Berl Schwartz for publicly calling him a demagogue.

Although it was impossible to prevent the motion from passing, the Jewish aldermen did accomplish something. They succeeded in having it softened. The overt anti-Semitic language was removed, leaving only the demand that, in view of the high unemployment in the country, the Liberal government shut the doors to immigration from Europe.

However, only in the city of Montreal was the resolution regarding the German Jews modified. In other cities and towns it was adopted in its original form, with words penned by anti-Semitic hands.

The Jewish Question in the Supreme Court

The Application for an Injunction against Anti-Semitic Newspapers.
The Historic Decision of Judge Desaulniers, an Indictment
against Anti-Semitism.

IN 1932 an attempt was made to stop the publication of anti-Semitic newspapers by means of a Superior Court injunction. This was in the same year that the Bercovitch bill to prohibit defamatory libel against a racial or ethnic group was defeated in the Quebec Legislature.[149]

A businessman from Lachine, E. Abugov, applied for an injunction against *Le Goglu* and *Le Miroir* on the grounds that as a member of the Jewish people, he personally had suffered damages because of the anti-Semitic libel promoted by Adrien Arcand and Joseph Ménard in their newspapers. This propaganda, he claimed, had induced anti-Semitic hooligans to throw stones at his store, smashing the windows. The lawyers for Mr. Abugov were Meyer Gameroff and Joseph Cohen,[150] then a member of the provincial legislature.

In the Jewish community a debate ensued as to whether the anti-Semites should be taken to court. Some people believed it would be more expedient to remain silent. This was the opinion of certain community leaders who maintained that taking legal action against the anti-Semites would make them into martyrs and ultimately win them more friends and supporters. Others argued that it would be impossible to find a judge or jury in all of Quebec to convict them. It would be more practical, they said, to refrain from legal proceedings. There was a large group, however, who claimed that it was wrong to be silent, that passivity would only serve to strengthen the influence of the anti-Semites, and their attitude toward the Jewish community would worsen.

By this time the Canadian Jewish Congress had been suspended. H. M. Caiserman, its first secretary, spoke in the name of the former Congress which would later need to be resurrected. In the meantime, the offices of the *Keneder Adler* had become the main centre for planning defensive strategies against the anti-Semites. Jewish lawyers, acting as individuals, participated in this activity, among them the Jewish members of the provincial legislature, Bercovitch[151] and Cohen, and S.W. Jacobs,[152] a member of the federal Parliament.

The Jewish community was in a state of agitation laced with fear. The news from Europe was alarming. In Germany, the Nazis were inching closer to taking over the reins of power, and the fate of the German Jews was practically sealed. In Poland, official anti-Semitism was on the rise. Jewish businesses were being squeezed and strangled by heavy taxes, and thugs were terrorizing Jewish students in the high schools and universities. Similar news was arriving from Rumania and Hungary. A catastrophe in Europe seemed imminent.

The application to the Superior Court for an injunction against the anti-Semitic publications was argued before Mr. Justice Desaulniers. After thorough deliberation, he rendered a lengthy judgment which came to be considered an historic document and one of the most important condemnations of anti-Semitism. However, there was no law pursuant to which the judge could order the injunction.

In his judgment, Mr. Justice Desaulniers regretted his inability to grant the application. He could, however, express the outrage of the court over the actions of the anti-Semites who claimed to be protecting the interests of French Canadians. This was not the case. The French inhabitants of Canada were a minority and it was against their interest to persecute another minority.

Mr. Justice Desaulniers incorporated a lengthy historical survey of anti-Semitism into his judgment, demonstrating that anti-Semitism was anti-Christian and immoral, and based on falsehoods, demagogy, and hypocrisy. Anti-Semitism was harmful not only to the Jews whom it victimized, but also to those in whose name it was propagated. The judge cited a French diplomat, a member of the Académie française and ambassador to Russia during the reign of the last tsar, who described the tragic situation of the Jews in Russia in 1915 during the First World War. After every defeat suffered by the Russian army, the tsarist police ordered severe reprisals against the Jews, mercilessly driving them from their homes. Later, when the execution of the tsar and his family took place in a cellar somewhere in Ekaterinenburg, did the innocent child, the heir to the throne, understand that he was paying for the sins of his fathers?[153]

The anti-Semitic campaign was also anti-Christian, Mr. Justice Desaulniers declared in his historic judgment. He quoted from Christian authorities to demonstrate the falseness of the accusations against the Talmud. In the strongest language he condemned the claims of Arcand and Ménard that the Talmud permitted the murder of Christians and the use of Christian blood for ritual purposes. The attacks against the Jews in *Le Miroir* and *Le Goglu* were comparable to the anti-Jewish propaganda disseminated by Drumont[154] in France which had caused deep divisions among the French, sapped their moral strength, and resulted in the banishment of an innocent man to Devil's Island.

The Jewish race, Mr. Justice Desaulniers emphasized, had shown that it was blessed with the capacity to outlive the empires which had enslaved it. Many of the nations which had oppressed the Jews had long ago ceased to exist. The judge stressed that he was introducing all these facts to express his concern as to why no law existed authorizing a judge to ban harmful propaganda of the type being disseminated by the anti-Semitic papers against the Jewish population.[155]

Mr. Justice Desaulniers was one of the first French Canadians to come out so forcefully against the anti-Semitic organizations in the province. This gave a great deal of encouragement to the Jewish community as well as to liberal circles in Quebec.

Although the judge was unable to grant the injunction, his written judgment, which attracted much attention in the general press, was very gratifying to the Jewish community.

Le Goglu, October 25, 1930
Bibliothèque nationale du Québec

The Defence of the Talmud in the Legislature

Henri Bourassa's Speech against the Anti-Semites. The Historic Speeches
of Peter Bercovitch and Joseph Cohen in the Legislature. The Splendid
Defence of the Talmud.

IN FEBRUARY OF 1932 the Bercovitch Bill was introduced in the Quebec
Legislature. Its aim was to remove the right of newspapers to print defamatory
or racist slander against Jews or any other group. By means of this bill the two
Jewish deputies, Peter Bercovitch and Joseph Cohen[156], hoped to avoid a direct
confrontation with the weeklies, *Le Miroir* and *Le Goglu*, over the aggressive
campaign they were conducting against the Jewish community. Their
publishers, Adrien Arcand and Joseph Ménard, were the leaders of the Nazi
movement in the Province of Quebec, and their influence was spreading to
other parts of Canada.

Mr. Bercovitch and Mr. Cohen had been re-elected to the Legislature in a
very nasty election campaign in the summer of 1931. The anti-Semitic Arcand
movement spared no effort in casting aspersion not only against the Jewish
candidates, but also against Premier Taschereau and other leaders of the Liberal
party for allowing members of the Jewish community to represent their party
in the provincial assembly.

The election of two Jewish representatives with large majorities was cause
for celebration in the Jewish community. The evening the results were
announced, thousands of Jews gathered in front of the *Keneder Adler* to express
their joy, not only because two Jews had been elected to the Legislature, but
also because the anti-Semitic campaign had failed to have any impact on the
majority of French Canadian voters.

A few days after the election, Henri Bourassa,[157] editor of *Le Devoir* and
intellectual leader of French Canadian nationalism, wrote an editorial voicing
his great satisfaction over the failure of the anti-Semitic campaign, supported
by certain Conservative leaders. In the same editorial, Mr. Bourassa praised
the position of Premier Taschereau, namely, that as long as the education of

children was entrusted to religious groups, Jewish parents could not be denied the right to control the education of their children, and keep it within the spirit of the Jewish faith.

Mr. Bourassa's stance against the anti-Semites was crucial, since he wielded considerable influence among French Canadian intellectuals. Known throughout the country as a leader of French Canadian nationalism, he was respected even by those who disagreed with his political views.

After their election to office, Mr. Bercovitch and Mr. Cohen considered it their duty to urge the Legislature to enact legislation prohibiting the printing of defamatory statements directed against any ethnic or religious group. To this end, the Bercovitch Bill was introduced and debated in February of 1932. The bill was not enacted into law. The Legislature contented itself with a resolution condemning anti-Semitic propaganda, but not prohibiting it. Opponents of the Bercovitch bill argued that it would restrict the freedom of the press.

Although the bill was defeated, the debate and the negotiations surounding it were important. They provided the opportunity for the two Jewish deputies to deliver speeches of historic significance, which received a great deal of attention in the entire country.

In his speech, Mr. Bercovitch warned that although the anti-Semitic movement targeted only Jews, its ultimate aim was to undermine the very basis of the democratic way of life in Canada. The Jewish population, he stated, was being put in a dangerous position by the provocations in the anti-Semitic press (*Le Goglu* and *Le Miroir*) which inflamed non-Jews with fallacious allegations that the Talmud allowed Jews to murder Christians and set fire to Christian houses. To put an end to this dangerous provocation, Mr. Bercovitch said, it was necessary to enact legislation protecting groups from defamation, just as existing law protected individuals.

Mr. Joseph Cohen dealt at length with the libellous attacks directed at the Talmud in the anti-Semitic papers, pointing out the calumnies employed by the anti-Semites to shame and debase the Jews in the eyes of their Christian neighbours. Mr. Cohen began his speech with the following dramatic words:

In 1832, exactly 100 years ago, this Legislature passed a law—twenty-five years before this was done in England—granting equal rights to all citizens of the Jewish faith. The bill was introduced by the immortal patriot Joseph Papineau[158] whose love of his own people did not blind him to the point of committing injustices against others, including the humble Jews who were then so few in number. His love of freedom erased all prejudices and religious differences which for hundreds of years had inspired anti-Semitic arguments. In this very Legislature those who heard Papineau's sincere voice voted the bill into law, catapulting the Province of Quebec into the forefront of all the enlightened countries of the world, and marking French Canadians as a nation that loves liberty.

One hundred years later, in 1932, the Jews of Quebec are standing in this same Legislature to ask the descendants of Louis-Joseph Papineau to protect them in the same spirit in which those rights were granted to them 100 years ago, to protect them from a movement designed to destroy the unity of the nation, to incite one segment of the population against the other, and to eradicate the rights and freedoms of minorities.[159]

The speeches of Mr. Bercovich and Mr. Cohen were highly praised and prominently reported in the non-Jewish press. This, however, did not deter the anti-Semitic groups. On the contrary, they were encouraged by the Legislature's refusal to enact the Bercovitch bill, and their activities intensified.

Among Liberal Journalists

The Role of *Le Canada* in the Struggle against Anti-Semitism. Meetings with Oliver Asselin and Edmonde Turcotte. Misunderstandings about Zionism in Liberal Circles.

FOR SOME TIME, the anti-Semitic movement led by the Arcand group encountered no opposition on the part of French Canadian journalists. Evidently there was a reluctance to confront Arcand and his friends. Finally, however, opposition appeared. It began with *Le Canada*,[160] a morning newspaper with close ties to the Liberal party.

This happened in 1933, the year Hitler became the chancellor of Germany. In Arcand's newspaper, *Le Miroir*, Hitler was a familiar figure. The same was true of Joseph Goebbels and Alfred Rosenberg, Hitler's "philosophers" and "intellectuals". However, of all the Nazis, Julius Streicher figured most prominently in Arcand's paper. The ancient diatribes against the Elders of Zion, the Talmud, *Kol Nidrei*, and so on, were regularly reprinted from Streicher's newspaper *Der Stürmer*.

Suddenly, in 1933, an editorial appeared in *Le Canada* roundly condemning Hitler's allies and supporters in the Province of Quebec, portraying them as liars, demagogues, and racketeers. The editorial had a strong impact. A few days earlier, a staff writer for *Le Canada*, Edmond Turcotte,[161] had alerted me to the fact that the editorial was about to be published. I would often meet Mr. Turcotte in the courthouse observing the trials, as I was also a court reporter for the *Keneder Adler*. As soon as the editorial appeared in print, it was translated into Yiddish and published in the *Keneder Adler*.

For the Jewish community, this was an important event. The editor of the *Adler*, Israel Rabinovitch,[162] immediately responded with an article warmly congratulating Mr. Asselin[163] for his courageous attack on Hitler's supporters in Quebec. I brought Rabinovitch's article, translated into English, to Mr. Asselin, to show him how much his editorial had been appreciated in the Yiddish newspaper. Mr. Asselin was delighted to see his article published in the Yiddish language. Among his friends, he said, was a priest who could read

Hebrew. Perhaps he would also be able to read the editorial in Yiddish.

Subsequent articles and editorials denouncing Quebec fascism appeared in *Le Canada*. They were written by both Mr. Asselin and Mr. Turcotte. Almost all of them were reprinted in translation in the *Keneder Adler*, with the result that close ties were established between the two newspapers. Occasionally Mr. Asselin would confer with Mr. Rabinovitch over the telephone on how best to combat the Jew-baiting in Canada and elsewhere.

In those days H. M. Caiserman,[164] secretary of the Canadian Jewish Congress, was extremely interested in making contact with French Canadians. He was known in the non-Jewish press as the representative of the Jewish community. Mr. Asselin once expressed the desire to meet him to discuss ways of fighting anti-Semitism in the Province of Quebec. One Friday afternoon I went with Caiserman to Mr. Asselin's office where a lengthy conversation ensued.

Caiserman had brought with him anti-Nazi brochures exposing Hitler and his followers as nothing more than gangsters and bandits. Asselin commented that this material did not answer a question that was troubling him. How was it possible that the German people, who had contributed so much to European culture and civilization, could treat the Jewish people so brutally? Could one really say that there had been no provocation whatsoever?

Asselin proceeded to answer his own question. Everywhere, he said, in times of crisis, all Jews, even powerful Jews, become vulnerable. This had happened in France at the time of Dreyfus, and was happening in Germany today. In times of upheaval, rage and bitterness are unleashed against the weak.

Caiserman agreed that Jewish weakness was a historic cause of anti-Semitism. Therefore he belonged to that segment of Jewish society which believed in Zionism. A Jewish state in Palestine would eliminate Jewish homelessness and vulnerability.

The conversation turned to Zionism. Asselin admitted that he knew nothing about Zionism other than what he had heard, namely, that wealthy Zionists were buying land from Arabs with the result that the Arabs were becoming poor and helpless. For this reason England now regretted having issued the Balfour Declaration. Was this true? Absolutely false, retorted Caiserman. Asselin said that he was curious to know the true facts.

From a drawer Asselin took a newspaper printed in France which contained an article about Zionism. The Jews, it stated, posed a grave danger for the Arabs, who were no match for the more adept Jewish merchants and financiers. In a short time Jews would transform Palestine into a country of commerce and industry, while the Arabs would be reduced to a source of cheap labour and even slave labour.

Caiserman stated, "Everything in that article is utterly false." He then described the Jewish farmers (*chalutzim*) and workers who were building the Land of Israel. They were struggling with all their might not against the Arabs, but against the swamps and deserts of a neglected country. These farmers and workers were among the most idealistic and ethical Jews.

"The Zionist movement," Caiserman continued, "was created by thinkers, philosophers, and intellectuals. Decades before the advent of Hitler, they already believed that Jewish powerlessness and homelessness would lead to pogroms, persecution and slaughter in times of international crises. The Arab masses will most certainly benefit from every point of view, financially as well as morally, when Palestine is developed through Jewish efforts. Their low standard of living will undoubtedly improve once they begin cooperating with the Jews instead of hindering them."

Asselin responded that what he had just heard about Zionism was very different from what he had previously believed. He was grateful for Caiserman's explanation.

In the 1930s, H.M. Caiserman advocated contact
with French Canadians.
Canadian Jewish Congress National Archives.

The Creation of the Second Jewish Congress

When Hitler Came to Power. The Boycott against German Goods.
The Revival of the Canadian Jewish Congress and Its Major Tasks
during the Hitler Period.

IN MARCH OF 1933 the Nazis came to power in Germany. Adolph Hitler became the Chancellor under President Hindenburg. This happened "legally" thanks to the elections one year earlier, when the Nazis became the largest party in the Reichstag. A week or two later the Nazis embarked on a campaign of terror against the Jews of Germany.

Grief and sorrow as well as a feeling of uncertainty gripped all the Jewish communities of the United States and Canada. Many people believed that democracy throughout the world was in decline.

Jewish businessmen in the United States and Canada were called upon to boycott all goods from Germany. In Montreal a committee was struck to direct the boycott and organize loud protests to arouse Canadian public opinion.

While some non-Jews had come to the realization that the Nazis posed a threat not only to Jews, but also to the Christian nations of Europe, others remained convinced that the Nazis intended to persecute only Jews and communists. Through their propaganda, the Nazis created the impression that their chief enemies were the Soviet Union and the Jewish people, and that with America, England, and France they would reach an understanding.

In April of 1933, a few weeks after the Nazis had assumed power in Germany, a large protest rally took place in Montreal in His Majesty's Theatre with the participation of prominent Christians. In addition to the mayor of Montreal, Fernand Rinfret, a well-known Liberal and educated man who acted as chairman, Bishop Farthing, head of the Protestant Church, and Raoul Dandurand, a banker, diplomat, and statesman, addressed the crowd.

This meeting attracted much attention. Senator Dandurand, Canada's representative at the League of Nations, was very knowledgeable about world politics. In his speech he described the political and economic circumstances leading to the Nazi takeover. He criticized the more powerful western nations for not dealing more leniently with previous German governments loyal to the Weimar constitution. Had they done so, he claimed, the Nazis in Germany and the fascists in Italy would never have come to power.

Soon after this meeting a new anti-Semitic organization was founded in Montreal by the name of *Le Jeune Canada*. This new organization convened a large gathering where the mayor of the city and Mr. Dandurand were attacked for interceding on behalf of the German Jews at the meeting in His Majesty's Theatre. Although young professionals and students joined this organization, there were other groups which condemned Nazi atrocities and barbarism. Within the Jewish community, there was a new sense that Jews were not alone in the struggle against Nazism.

Public opinion in Canada, as in the United States, had become exceedingly alarmed over the danger of Nazism. Nazi groups began to spring up everywhere. These groups, under various names, could be found throughout the United States. A few of their leaders appeared regularly in the daily newspapers. Most prominent of all was Father Coughlin of Detroit. Another familiar name was Fritz Kuhn, leader of the organization "Bund" formed by Americans of German descent. In both the United States and Canada the official representatives of Germany, the German embassies and consulates, became centres for the dissemination of anti-Semitic Nazi propaganda.

On the other hand, groups of anti-fascists were organized to conduct a vigorous campaign—through education, of course—against Nazism. Large groups of students, professors, journalists, artists, and, generally speaking, the leading intellectuals in the United States and Canada joined these groups. From the outset, the trade union movement had identified with the struggle against Nazism. Union leaders in the United States and Canada proclaimed publicly that Nazis and fascists were the mortal enemies of organized labour. In Canada, at a time when most groups were calling for the government to bar any further immigration from Europe, the Canadian Trades and Labour Congress demanded on a number of occasions that Canada open its doors to all Jewish victims of the Nazi regime. In the spring of 1933, after the rally in His Majesty's Theatre, pressure to revive the Canadian Jewish Congress intensified. People had become aware that the fight against Nazism had to be conducted on a massive scale, and that large sums would have to be raised in order to be able to assist German Jews who had already begun fleeing Germany to escape the bloody catastrophe which now appeared to be inevitable.

Throughout 1933 various conferences were held in Montreal, Toronto, and Winnipeg, to plan the resurrection of the Canadian Jewish Congress. No longer was there any opposition. All the various political and cultural currents in Jewish life were united in the rescue effort.

The plenary session of the second Canadian Jewish Congress opened in October of 1934. This was certainly an historic event. The most urgent item on the agenda was, of course, the situation of the Jews in Germany. Anti-Semitic persecution was also rampant in countries such as Poland, Rumania, and Hungary. It appeared as though several governments were conspiring to annihilate the Jews of Europe.

At the second session of the Canadian Jewish Congress, S. W. Jacobs[165] was elected president. His position as a member of the federal Parliament was crucial in defending Jewish rights and dignity. H. M. Caiserman[166] was elected secretary.

The creation of the second Jewish Congress inaugurated a new chapter of nation-wide coordinated Jewish activity in various spheres.

The Doctors' Strike against the Jews

Interns at the Notre Dame Hospital Strike against the Hiring of a Jewish Doctor.
Difficulties for Jewish Doctors. Opening of the Jewish Hospital.

IN 1934 all the Yiddish and English-language newspapers were full of grim news about the brutal persecution of the Jews of Germany. Reading such news was horrifying. It seemed that the German people had slid from the heights of civilization into a morass of mediaeval barbarism. Many people in the United States and Canada predicted that this was the tragic end of European culture and civilization.

There were reports about the burning of books authored by Jewish writers and thinkers. With great fanfare the works of Professor Einstein, Emile Ludwig, Lion Feuchtwanger, and many other first-class novelists, poets, playwrights, and scientists were publicly incinerated. All the libraries in every single town and city in Germany were purged of these books.

In 1934 the actions of anti-Semites everywhere became more overt, aggressive, and violent. They did their utmost to demonstrate their support for the Nazis and poison the air with Nazi propaganda against the Jewish population. That same year, the anti-Semitic movement in the Province of Quebec, led by the Arcand gang, broadened its activities and infiltrated various social circles, including young professionals, lawyers, and doctors.

During a trial in the Superior Court, a young lawyer objected to an oath taken by a Jew. Quoting from the *Kol Nidrei*, the lawyer argued that this holy prayer, which Jews recite on the eve of Yom Kippur, the Day of Atonement, allowed Jews to give false testimony against Christians in a court of law. Mr. Justice MacKinnon, in overruling the objection, reprimanded the lawyer for repeating anti-Semitic libel used by enemies of the Jews in the Middle Ages to persecute Jewish communities. In the course of his attack on the *Kol Nidrei*, the lawyer had revealed that he was a reader of Arcand's anti-Semitic publications which featured the same sort of calumnies against the Jews. Other lawyers, on a number of occasions, also demonstrated their hatred of Jews and satisfaction with Hitler's savage treatment of the Jewish communities of Germany.

That same year, 1934, the anti-Semitic strike of the young doctors at the Notre Dame Hospital attracted a great deal of attention. The strike broke out over the hiring of a young Jewish doctor as an intern. The other interns demanded that he be dismissed, and when the administration refused, they called a strike. The young doctors picketed the hospital, ensuring that there were no strike-breakers.

The strike stirred public opinion, and the strikers were condemned from every quarter. As news of the strike spread throughout Canada and into the United States, Dr. Rabinovitch,[167] who was at the centre of this conflict, was offered work in various American and Canadian hospitals as an intern. Within the Jewish community there was disagreement as to whether he should resign from the Notre Dame Hospital, or remain there. Many were of the opinion that, for the sake of peace, he should resign and thus save the hospital administration from any further embarrassment. Others believed that he should remain at the hospital to avoid encouraging anti-Semitic gangs in their harassment of the Jewish population. There were also Christians who believed that the Jewish doctor should not resign, so as not to give satisfaction to the anti-Semites.

Finally, Dr. Rabinovitch did, in fact, resign, and the anti-Semites interpreted this as a victory. The Jewish community was pleased that French Canadian public opinion, the French press, well-known Quebec political leaders, and a large part of the intelligentsia, had condemned the strikers. It turned out that the strike had been instigated by a handful of young men, influenced by the powerful anti-Semitic propaganda disseminated at that time.[168]

In this connection, it is important to note that in those years it was quite difficult, in general, for young Jewish doctors to obtain an internship in a Montreal hospital. As very few were accepted, many Jewish graduates had to leave Montreal for jobs in the United States where it was much easier to find a position in a hospital. The situation began to improve in 1934, the year the Jewish Hospital opened in Montreal.

The construction of the Jewish Hospital was a major event in the Jewish community. The need for this facility was pressing, not only for Jewish patients, but also for Jewish doctors, both young and old, who lacked a medical institution where they could feel at home and not like outsiders.

The initiative to build a Jewish hospital in Montreal came in 1928 from a group of downtown Jews with the active support of H. Wolofsky[169] and the *Keneder Adler*. That year was one of prosperity, and it seemed that raising the necessary funds would not present any problems. However, in 1929, with the failure of the stock market, it became difficult to collect the required amount. This serious obstacle was later overcome, however, thanks to the Bronfman brothers who assumed the leadership of a large fundraising campaign. When Mr. Alan Bronfman took charge of the hospital building project, its success was assured. For a long time he remained the president of the hospital, and under his administration it developed into one of the most modern medical institutions in Montreal.

Pastry chef, Mr. A. Kuneges, prepares for
Coronation Day, May 12, 1937 at Montreal's
Jewish General Hospital.
Courtesy of Ellie Moidel

Catholic Syndicates and Jewish Unions

The Struggle of the Catholic Syndicates against the "Jewish"
Needle-Trade Unions. The Crisis in the Clothing Workers' Unions.
The Dramatic Dressmakers' Strike.

IN THE TUMULTUOUS period of the 1930s, when factional strife weakened the needle trade unions, the Catholic syndicates made a concerted effort to infiltrate the clothing industries. It was their aim to drive out the two giant unions, the Amalgamated and the International.[170]

The leaders of the Catholic syndicates attacked the needle trade unions, claiming that they were headed by communists and therefore harmful to the Catholic province. In this campaign, assisted by the anti-Semitic newspapers distributed in Quebec by the Arcand group, they completely ignored the fact that the leaders of the International and the Amalgamated were then engaged in a bitter struggle against the influence of communism in the trade union movement.

At this time the Catholic syndicates were under the direction of the Catholic Church. Their main objective was to organize French Canadian workers into religious unions to prevent them from joining the international unions, which were affiliates of American unions. The syndicates had kept their distance from the workers in the clothing industry, taking into account the fact that most of them were Jewish and hence not their territory.[171]

Nevertheless, in the 1930s, under the influence of the anti-Semitic movement, the Catholic syndicates believed the time was ripe for undermining the "Jewish" unions to gain control over the many workers who were employed in the needle trades. They appealed especially to the Christians who worked in these industries. Since they had to negotiate with Jewish manufacturers the Catholic syndicates refrained from using overtly anti-Semitic slogans. To the Jewish factory owners they proposed contracts with low wages. They also assured them that once under the control of the Catholic syndicates, the tailors would not strike. This was a sincere promise. Everyone knew that Catholic syndicates were against such tactics as strikes.

A number of manufacturers accepted the offer of the Catholic unions, believing that it would enable them to force the International, which was just beginning to recover from the crisis caused by internal wrangling, to leave Montreal. The two large unions in Montreal's needle trades were ruined by these factional quarrels. For a long time the Cloakmakers' Union ceased to function. For its members this precipitated a serious crisis. The factory owners had taken advantage of the situation to drive wages down to the minimum with the result that many families of cloakmakers were forced to accept charity.

The tailors in the men's clothing industry had their own problems. A group of them had revolted against the Amalgamated and created a competing union in which the leftists were the initiators and the driving force. For a while the new organization, calling itself the Canadian Union, controlled the workers and won a collective agreement from the manufacturers who were happy to see the Amalgamated in trouble. But the tailors were soon disillusioned with the poor working conditions and returned to their old union. The Amalgamated had been in operation the entire time with a rather small number of loyal members who had paid their dues even when they had been compelled to pay dues to the Canadian Union as well, in order to keep their jobs. These loyal tailors were the "right-wing" socialists and the Poalei Zionists. They joined forces in order to protect the Amalgamated against the "left-wing" union.

The defunct Cloakmakers Union was resuscitated thanks to a small group of loyal members who had waited for an opportunity to reopen the union office. Among the leaders of this group was Albert Eaton,[172] who for a long time played an important role in the Montreal International, and afterwards became the administrator of the Joint Commission of the Cloaks Industry. To help this group in its efforts to reinvigorate the Cloakmakers Union, the head office sent Bernard Shane[173], who was then a special organizer. Within a short time, Mr. Shane, now the vice-president of the International, reorganized the cloakmakers who had become alienated from that union.

After the Cloakmakers' Union was revived, Mr. Shane began a campaign to organize the dressmakers. This was in the mid-1930s when Montreal was an important centre for the dress industry. Although most of the workers were French Canadian girls and women who had never been members of a union, the International had no difficulty in organizing the female workers. Problems arose only when the manufacturers refused to conclude a collective agreement with the union. The International then proclaimed a strike, which created a great deal of tension in the Montreal garment district. This dramatic strike lasted for several weeks, and ended in a decisive victory for the International.[174]

It was during this strike that the Catholic syndicates intervened in an attempt to prevent French Canadian workers from joining a "Jewish" union. They accused the leaders of the International in New York and Montreal of being either overt or covert communists. The French Canadian workers, however, rejected this propaganda, and demonstrated their loyalty to the International which spoke to them in the name of liberalism and inter-racial solidarity, and against the exploitation and oppression of workers.

The Catholic syndicates are now an important force in the Province of Quebec. In recent years they have made significant progress and are far less reactionary than they were in the 1930s.

The Trial against Anti-Semitism in Ottawa

A Detective Who Engaged in Anti-Semitism. Zionism and the
Talmud at the Trial Initiated by the President of the Zionist Organization.

THE MILITANT ANTI-SEMITIC movement in the Province of Quebec led by the
National Christian Social Party crossed over into parts of Ontario, including
Ottawa, the country's capital, where it acquired a few adherents.

A well-known police detective took it upon himself "to drive the Jews out
of Ottawa". He began with a campaign to boycott Jewish businesses in Ottawa
and its vicinity. To achieve this Nazi-like objective, the detective, Jean Tissot,
imported anti-Semitic literature from Montreal and elsewhere, which he
distributed in the capital, and recruited a group of people to help him in this
work. At the same time, he approached non-Jewish businessmen to ask for
financial support for his boycott campaign against stores run by Jews.

Detective Tissot targeted the large department store owned by Archie
Freiman who was then the national president of the Canadian Zionist Organization. He distributed a pamphlet singling out the Freimans, and naming
Freiman as one of the most prominent leaders of Canadian Jewry and responsible for collecting Canadian money to send to the Land of Israel. He called
upon Christians in the Ottawa area to boycott Freiman's store. In a Jewish
store, Tissot claimed, a customer is not treated honestly. He sent the leaflet to
Christian businessmen, expecting them to reward him well for it.

The leaflet, however, did not work to his advantage. In Ottawa such villainy
was soon halted. First Tissot was dismissed from the police force. Then he was
tried in a court of law. Mr. Freiman had accused him of defamation.

The trial attracted attention throughout the country. In Montreal, Arcand's
anti-Semitic newspapers immediately declared Tissot a martyr and victim of
Jewish persecution. In the general press, Freiman was applauded for taking
such prompt legal action to nip the Ottawa anti-Semitic movement in the
bud. By this time Mr. Freiman was known in Ottawa, as well as the rest of
Canada, as a Jewish leader. His wife was renowned and respected not only as

president of Hadassah, but also for her humanitarian activities on behalf of Jewish and other welfare institutions.

The trial, which took place in the fall of 1935 before a judge and jury, was very dramatic. The defendant sought to play the role of a man being persecuted for being a good patriot and fighting for his land and nation against "the enemies of Christendom". The Crown attorney described him as a racketeer, a charlatan, and a slanderer. The following facts, among others, were presented as evidence. The defendant had gone to the large department store of Bryson-Graham to request a financial contribution for his anti-Semitic work. He spoke with two of the people in charge, Mr. William Graham, the store's vice-president, and Mr. G. Monroe, the treasurer and manager. Tissot proposed that they become members of his League for Christian Store Owners Against Jews. This league had undertaken to organize a boycott of Jewish businesses with the objective of driving Jewish storeowners out of Ottawa and thereby freeing Christian merchants and shopkeepers from Jewish competitors.

To prove that the league was doing its work effectively, Detective Tissot showed them a leaflet distributed by the league against Jewish shopkeepers. It contained an article formerly published in the Montreal newspaper *Le Patriote*, one of Arcand's anti-Semitic organs. The article was a vicious attack on the Freimans with slanderous allegations against the management of the Freiman Store in Ottawa. This fact was brought out in court. Both Mr. Graham and Mr. Monroe appeared as witnesses for the prosecution.

Mr. Freiman also testified at the trial. Tissot's lawyer tried to discredit him on the grounds that he, Freiman, was a prominent figure in the Zionist leadership. The lawyer attempted to create the impression that Zionism was a movement of "international Jewry" which aimed to exploit the poor Arab peasants in Palestine and deprive them of their land.

Freiman outlined to the jury the basic aims of the Zionist movement in Canada and elsewhere. The ultimate objective, he explained, was to create a homeland for several million Jews and give them the opportunity to revive Jewish culture and create a modern civilization. The Arab masses, he argued, would benefit greatly if Palestine were to be transformed by Jews into a civilized and developed country.

Tissot's lawyer asked Mr. Freiman to explain the aims of the Talmud. Was it true that the Talmud allowed Jews to cheat Christians and swindle them in business? Mr. Freiman replied that these allegations against the Talmud were thoroughly false and that attacking the Talmud was one of the vilifications used by anti-Semites in their war against the Jews.

The jury heard the arguments of the lawyers for both sides and came to the conclusion that Tissot was guilty of defamatory libel. In the end he was allowed to get away with paying a fine.[175]

A.J. Freiman
The Jew in Canada (Jewish Publications Ltd.), 1926.

The Attack on the Quebec City Synagogue

The Attempt to Prevent the Construction of a New Synagogue in Quebec City.
The Fire in the Synagogue on the Eve of Its Inauguration.
Tension in the Community.

IN THE 1930S the militant anti-Semitism originating in Montreal spread to Quebec City where a few groups were actively engaged in inciting the population against the local Jewish community. The anti-Semitic newspapers published by Adrien Arcand and printed in Montreal were distributed in Quebec City. There the most active group was Achat Chez Nous, supported by the influential newspaper *L'Action catholique*.

At the same time, the Quebec Jewish community had decided to construct a new synagogue, larger and more impressive than the existing one. The old synagogue had been built by immigrant Jews who were mostly peddlers and small businessmen. Members of the second generation, having worked their way up the economic ladder, now undertook to erect a larger synagogue building in a fine residential neighbourhood. The purchase of a lot by the Jewish community for the new synagogue building caused a stir in certain Christian circles. They vehemently protested that only private homes, not public buildings, could be constructed in that neighbourhood. When Jewish community leaders chose to ignore this outcry, the opposition hurried to the courts to seek an injunction to prevent the Jewish community from building the synagogue. However, the opposition was unsuccessful, a building permit was obtained, and work commenced.

Nevertheless, the agitation which had begun in the 1930s against the synagogue continued unabated. The climax came in May of 1944, mid-way through the construction. On a Saturday night, after preparations had been completed for the inauguration of the building the following day, anti-Semitic hooligans set fire to the completed basement, causing severe damage.

The question immediately arose as to whether to proceed with the inauguration or postpone it. A decision was taken to begin repairs at once and carry on with the celebration as planned. The ceremony took place on a Sunday afternoon. The synagogue was filled to capacity with people of all ages, men, women, and children. Among them were a few young men in uniform. The atmosphere was as solemn as Yom Kippur eve as the cantor chanted a prayer with a mournful melody. In his speech Rabbi Mednick[176] emphasized the gravity of the fire set the previous night.

The mood changed, however, in the evening, at the inauguration banquet. It appeared that the Jews of Quebec City had indeed come to celebrate. They congratulated one another and wished each other *mazel tov*. Seated at the head table along with the banquet chairmen, Sydney Lazarovitch and O. Miller, were a number of prominent community leaders from Montreal representing the Canadian Jewish Congress.

Mr. Miller, the president of the synagogue, noted that although the fire had been a painful disappointment, it had also had the positive effect of uniting the younger generation with their parents. It was a pleasure to see how the youth had come to the synagogue immediately after the fire to help clean up and repair the damage. The young people had requested that the celebration not be postponed so as not to give the impression that its opponents had won a victory.

Morris Pollack,[177] chairman of the building committee, noted that although such incidents were extremely painful, Jewish history was filled with anti-Jewish attacks throughout the ages, throughout the world. Jews had to have faith in God, and not lose their trust in French Quebecers, who were fundamentally honest, hard-working, God-fearing, and hospitable. The anti-Semitic thugs who mouthed Hitler's words were speaking a foreign tongue, in an alien spirit, not the language and spirit of French Canadians.

A Stormy Election Campagin

Anti-Semites Run in the Federal Elections and Lose. Jewish Members of
Parliament during the Critical Years of the 1930s.

IN THE AUTUMN of 1935 federal elections took place in Canada. The anti-Semites ran a boisterous campaign on two fronts, in Montreal and in Ottawa.

Their candidate in Montreal, Salluste Lavery, a lawyer and bitter enemy of the Jewish people, was challenging S. W. Jacobs, Member of Parliament since 1917. This was the same Lavery, who a few years earlier had run for mayor in the Montreal municipal elections. During that campaign he promised the voters that once elected he would concentrate all his efforts on a single objective—to protect the Canadian metropolis from the "Jewish menace". He was, of course, defeated, but he won a significant number of votes.

During the federal campaign Lavery left no stone unturned in his effort to incite against the Jewish community and Jews in general. Lavery convened large gatherings at which the only issue addressed was the fight against the Jews. A wide range of speakers, mostly unknown professionals, ranted and raved that Canada was being threatened by a "Jewish conspiracy". This conspiracy consisted of trying to draw Canada into the war against Germany for the purpose of interceding on behalf of the Jews there. If Jacobs were re-elected to Parliament, they argued, he would most certainly drag Canada into a war for the sake of the Jewish people.

These same speakers justified the Nazi persecution of Jews. All the Jews of Germany were communists who wanted to destroy Christian civilization and assist the Bolsheviks in their drive to dominate the whole of Europe. With this propaganda they would inflame the audience, which included quite a few young people. Arcand's anti-Semitic newspapers, along with other anti-Jewish material, were either sold or distributed free of charge at these meetings.

The campaign rallies organized by Jacobs were attended by prominent Canadian personalities including well-known lawyers and even members of the federal cabinet who, in their speeches, called upon French Canadian voters to condemn the anti-Semitic tirades at the Lavery meetings. They underlined the fact that the pro-Nazi speeches of Lavery and his friends were contrary to the Christian and humanitarian spirit of French Canada. They urged people to vote for Jacobs in order to demonstrate that the Province of Quebec belonged to the Christian world and was not sympathetic to the barbaric Nazis.

This election campaign captured much attention in both Jewish and non-Jewish circles and ended in a resounding victory for Jacobs. Lavery did not win a significant number of votes, not even in the streets where French Canadians lived. After that campaign little was heard from him again.

In Ottawa the anti-Semites put forward as their candidate the former detective Jean Tissot, who had already earned a reputation as a first-class fascist. This was the same Tissot who had previously instigated an anti-Semitic campaign in Ottawa, in particular against A. J. Freiman, president of the Canadian Zionist Organization and owner of a large department store. As a result, Tissot had been prosecuted for criminal libel and found guilty, but escaped with a light penalty.

Tissot conducted a clamorous campaign. He appealed to the voters to send him to Parliament so that he could fight the Jews whom he accused of wanting to inundate the country with Jewish refugees from Germany and Austria. This was the first time that an openly anti-Semitic election campaign took place in Ottawa. Tissot received a mere 4,000 votes, in comparison to the 16,000 of his Liberal (non-Jewish) opponent.

In this election, in addition to Mr. Jacobs, two Jews, Samuel Factor,[178] a Liberal from Toronto, and A. A. Heaps,[179] a socialist from Winnipeg, were voted into office.

An Anti-Semitic Meeting in a Church

Leaders of the Anti-Semitic Movement Prepare to Govern a "Fascist Canada".
A Promise to Punish Certain Jewish Leaders Once in Power.

As THE NAZIS gained momentum in Germany, the anti-Semitic gangs in Montreal and in the Province of Quebec as a whole, became more aggressive and militant. At the same time it became apparent that opposition to them was growing. It reached the point where order had to be strictly enforced at anti-Semitic rallies to prevent riots. At one of the largest such gatherings, in the spring of 1938, a brawl erupted. Members of the crowd had been heckling the speakers with shouts of "dirty fascists!" People had asked questions without receiving satisfactory replies, questions about the relationship of the Nazis to the Catholic Church. When the questioners became too persistent, an attempt was made to eject them from the hall. A fistfight ensued, putting an end to the meeting. The Nazis then accused the Jews and communists of trying to disrupt their meetings.

At that time it was rumoured that certain priests, either directly or indirectly, supported the anti-Semitic activities of the Arcand gang. One day, in *Le Fasciste canadien*, one of Arcand's newspapers, there was an announcement of an important meeting to be held in the auditorium of the St. Thomas Aquinas Catholic Church on Convent Street with an invitation for everyone to come and hear what was happening in the world and how the battle against "Jewish domination" was progressing.

When I saw the notice, I decided to attend the meeting, even if it involved some personal risk. I entered the hall without attracting any attention. About 1,000 people were present at this meeting which lasted about three hours.

Adrien Arcand was the main speaker. His tone conveyed his complete certainty that fascism was spreading throughout the entire world, that everything created by the Jews—democracy, liberalism, communism, and capitalism—was collapsing; that England and France would certainly be won over to national-socialism; that Canada would also soon become a fascist state;

that his party was preparing to take over the reins of government; and, when this happened, all problems would be resolved and the Jews would not be able to drag Canada into a war with Germany.

The second speaker was Major Scott,[180] Arcand's "military expert", who described Canada's future as a fascist state. He was expected to train and prepare an army of "storm troopers" to help Arcand's party come to power in Canada. The chairman, Dr. Gabriel Lambert, a dentist, declared himself ready to abandon his profession in order to assume a ministerial post when Arcand became prime minister.

The meeting was attended by approximately 300 young men and women in special uniforms to indicate their membership in Arcand's Nazi party. They distributed anti-Semitic pamphlets and brochures to the audience, including a thick brochure entitled "La clef du mystère" (The Key to the Mystery). This brochure, written by Dr. Lambert, was widely circulated throughout the province. It contained excerpts from the *Protocols of the Elders of Zion* and other anti-Semitic material.

For me the atmosphere in the hall was heavy and oppressive. While portraits of the saints adorned the walls, from the podium fire and brimstone were spewed against Jews all over the world. I felt as though I was not in Montreal, but in some city in Germany. It occurred to me that this was probably how people spoke in the Middle Ages at the time of the Inquisition. I regretted having come here. A few people got up and left the hall. I, too, wanted to leave but was afraid I might be recognized while making my way to the door. It seemed safer for me to sit quietly in my seat.

Arcand's speech was longer than the others. After providing an overview of the general world situation, he described how all countries were now preparing for eventual National Socialist rule. Then he raised the question of how the Jews of Canada should be dealt with once his party came to power. Would the Jews be expelled from the country?

Arcand said no. This he would certainly not do! It would be more practical, he said, for them to remain in this country to be persecuted and tormented as in Germany and Austria. Arcand called out the names of a number of Jewish leaders with whom special accounts would need to be settled. He mentioned the names of A. J. Freiman, president of the Canadian Zionists, Rabbi H. Stern[181] of Temple Emanu-El, and H. M. Caiserman of the Jewish Congress. They would all be sent at once to Bordeaux Prison for hard labour.

Although in 1938 the Arcand gang held many meetings in Montreal and other parts of Quebec, and even outside the province, the one I attended received special attention because it took place in a church. The Jewish community was curious to know if Catholic officials had prior knowledge of this meeting. A subsequent report revealed that a low-level functionary had rented out the church hall without asking permission from his superiors.

As I have mentioned, in those days there was already strong opposition to Arcand's Nazi movement. Many French-language newspapers, both dailies and weeklies, warned that the Nazis in Germany and their sympathizers in Canada were a danger not only to Jews, but also to Christians. They alerted readers to the massive rearmament taking place in Germany with the slogan "guns instead of butter", which could end up costing the lives of millions of people in the democratic countries.

In other parts of Canada the Nazis had no influence at all. There were Nazi groups here and there, but they were not able to attract a strong following.

A meeting of Adrien Arcand's Nazi movement, Montreal, 1938.

Fascism vs Democracy

The World Situation in 1938. Premier Duplessis Regrets His Anti-Semitism. My Dramatic Interview with Him. Louis Fitch in the Quebec Legislature.

BY 1938 a majority of Canada's political leaders, like those in other countries, knew that the German Nazis were planning a war to enable the "Aryan supreme race" to gain control of a large part of the world, and perhaps the entire globe.

In the powerful nations— the United States, England, France, and the Soviet Union—plans for a defensive strategy in the event of a Nazi attack were already underway. Some Western political leaders then believed that a settlement could still be reached with Hitler. For this purpose Prime Minister Chamberlain of England and Prime Minister Daladier of France travelled to Munich where they negotiated a treaty meant to ensure peace for the Western nations. The Munich Agreement ended in tragedy, and indirectly led to the Second World War.

Some political leaders, who had previously displayed pro-fascist leanings, realized on the eve of World War II that their sympathies had been misplaced. They made an effort to reverse their positions and stay on a more or less democratic course. Premier Duplessis,[182] who had harboured pro-fascist sympathies at the beginning of the 1930s, by 1938 began to show a change of heart. Uncomfortable over the fact that he had been characterized as an enemy of the Jews, he wanted to repair his image in the Jewish community. To this end, he invited the well-known Zionist and community leader Louis Fitch[183] to be the Union Nationale candidate in the St. Louis district. A by-election had become necessary because Peter Bercovich had resigned his seat in the Quebec Legislature in order to run for federal Parliament.

Some Jewish groups were unhappy that Louis Fitch had agreed to be a candidate for the party of Duplessis. Mr. Fitch then explained that he had done so because he believed first of all, that Duplessis was truly repentant, and secondly, that as an insider, he could have some impact on the Union Nationale members of the Legislature who were still under the influence of the anti-Semitic propaganda which had swayed them in earlier years.

Part of the Jewish community supported Fitch. Backing him was the *Keneder Adler*, which called upon Jews to give Fitch their full confidence and their votes. The newspaper counselled that it would be useful for the Jews to have Fitch in the Legislature.

Before the election campaign the *Keneder Adler* received a request to print a declaration from Premier Duplessis clarifying his position with regard to the Jews. I was sent to interview him. The conversation took place in the Premier's Montreal office, which was then a suite in the Mount Royal Hotel.

When I arrived, the Premier already had a prepared typed statement in English, in which he gave assurances that he was not an enemy of the Jews. On the contrary, he respected the Jewish community and had a number of Jewish friends whose friendship he valued.

I was somewhat taken aback when the Premier asked me what I thought of this declaration. He told me that he was very interested in hearing my opinion. In response, I told him that I could not speak for the newspaper, but could only give him my personal opinion. My opinion, however, might not be shared by the Jewish community as a whole. "For me personally," I said, "it is not very important whether or not you are friendly to the Jews. For me it is important to know if you are a supporter of the democratic constitution under which we live and find protection here in Canada. If you are not a supporter of the constitution, then we cannot rely on you, even if you have Jews among your friends."

This remark provoked a lengthy conversation which lasted for over an hour. During our discussion, the Premier spoke about the situation in the world, especially in Europe. He told me that as a devout Catholic he was very concerned about the future. He feared that the future belonged to Hitler and Mussolini, who were gaining ground and spreading their influence all over the world.

The Premier stressed the fact that he could not be a supporter of Hitler and Mussolini because what they were doing was contrary to the spirit of Catholicism. But the Nazis were very strong and making further gains. Sooner or later they would take over all of Europe and beyond. The situation was tragic. Certainly, for the Jews, it was deplorable, but what could be done? With the constitutional democracies in their present state, the rise of fascism could not be stopped. It was impossible!

After he had clearly stated his point of view, he asked whether I was in agreement with his "objective and realistic" assessment of the general situation in Europe. "No, Mr. Premier," I replied, "I think you are underestimating the power of anti-fascist sentiment shared by people all over the world who are prepared to fight against the dark forces of Hitlerism."

The Premier said that he had recently visited London and Paris where he had conferred with top political leaders. They had told him it was impossible to stop the power of fascism. He again emphasized that he felt a great deal of compassion for the Jews of Europe whose future looked very bleak.

I thanked him for expressing sympathy for the Jews, but informed him that the Jewish people were not the only ones at risk. Tragedy awaited the French, the Belgians, and even perhaps the British. Hitler was not preparing a powerful army to use against Jews. Jews could be destroyed without a Luftwaffe and without tanks.

"If there is a war, it will be against the communists, against Russia, not against France," the Premier asserted with conviction.

Premier Duplessis was polite, even when I said that I completely disagreed with him. He replied that time would prove him right.

In those days one often met political leaders who claimed that even though they were against the Nazis, they believed the Nazis would eventually become a great world power and we would have to adapt to their rule. They took a kind of "co-existence" approach to fascism and Nazism. Evidently Mr. Duplessis was one of them. In the meantime, he wanted to show that he was not an adherent of Nazi ideology whose main objective was war against the Jews.

When it became known that Duplessis had nominated Fitch as a candidate for the Legislature, a sizeable delegation of his party members and sympathizers presented him with a petition containing a long list of signatures demanding that he rescind the nomination. He rejected their demand, stating that he respected the rights of the Jewish minority in the Province of Quebec.

Fitch was elected to office. When he entered the Legislature, Duplessis appeared very friendly to him. Very soon after taking his seat Fitch had the opportunity to deliver a speech in the Legislature which made a strong impression and received a great deal of attention in the liberal French press. Addressing the issue of Jewish-Christian relations, Fitch highly praised the spirit of tolerance and friendship manifested by French Canadians vis-à-vis the Jewish minority. He reminded his listeners that one hundred years earlier, the Quebec Legislature had first enacted legislation granting equal rights to Jews.[184]

The provincial election was held in 1939. Duplessis was defeated and the Liberals formed a government under the leadership of Adélard Godbout.[185] In the St. Louis district, Fitch also lost his seat to Maurice Hartt.[186]

The main issue during the election campaign had been the rearmament of Canada. It was already clear that the Nazis posed a danger not only for Jews, and not only for communists, but for the entire Western world. Nevertheless, Duplessis had campaigned in favour of "limited" preparation for war, and for this was reason his party lost the election.

Poster, 1938, advertising a rally for Louis Fitch, federal candidate in Montreal's St. Louis district.
Canadian Jewish Congress National Archives.

After Kristallnacht

The Beginning of Terrorism against German Jews. The Night That Shook the
Jewish World. The Protest Meeting. At a Mass Meeting of Montreal Nazis.

IN THE AUTUMN of 1938, the tragic news from Germany horrified every Jew,
as well as liberal circles in the United States and Canada. It was now obvious
that the Nazis were preparing actual pogroms. After the Munich Agreement,
they believed they could do whatever they wanted regardless of world opinion.
Although the Nazis had never been overly concerned with public opinion in
the past, after the British Prime Minister Chamberlain and his French counter-
part Daladier had signed the Appeasement Pact, they became even bolder and
much more brutal than ever before in their treatment of Jews.

The campaign of terror began on the night of November 9, 1938—
Kristallnacht. That night Nazi storm troopers attacked and plundered Jewish
homes, set fire to 273 synagogues, destroyed 7,500 Jewish businesses, and threw
20,000 Jews into concentration camps.

When this was reported, sadness settled over the Jewish community. People
felt as though the world was coming to an end. Until now they had believed
that the Germans would content themselves with discrimination, humiliation,
and exclusionary laws. No one imagined that they would burn synagogues
and resort to atrocities and violence on a massive scale.

In the United States and Canada, Jewish leaders did not know what to do.
They felt that they could not keep silent; at the very least they had to rally in
protest. The Canadian Jewish Congress immediately organized gigantic demonstrations all over the country. The largest were held simultaneously in
Montreal and Toronto on Sunday, November 20, 1938.

In Toronto 16,000 Jews met at Maple Leaf Gardens under the chairmanship
of A. B. Bennett[187], a distinguished leader in the Canadian Jewish Congress.
Addressing the crowd were prominent Protestant and Catholic clergy, as well
as high-profile politicians. It was one of the largest Jewish rallies ever held in
Toronto.

The Montreal demonstration took place in His Majesty's Theatre. The hall was filled to capacity. Thousands of people who could not get in stood outside on a nearby empty lot. Jews of every political, religious, and cultural affiliation, including those who seldom participated in Jewish meetings, were in attendance. The atmosphere was as solemn as on *Tisha b'av*.[188] The pupils of the Jewish schools also participated in this mournful event.

The chairman, Chief Justice Greenshield, opened the meeting by declaring that the Nazis had brought back to Europe the barbarism of the Middle Ages. He said that the entire civilized world, including Canada, was obligated to intervene on behalf of the Jewish people.

Among the other speakers at this historic meeting were Benjamin Robinson, K.C.,[189] Rabbi H. Abramovitz[190] of the Sha'ar Hashamayim Synagogue, Rabbi H. Stern[191] of the Temple Emanu-el, and a few influential Christians. Every speaker called upon Canada to open its gates at once to the Jewish refugees from Germany. This demand was repeated at all the protest rallies taking place throughout Canada.

Demonstrations were held in various cities in the United States. President Franklin D. Roosevelt recalled the American ambassador from Berlin in protest. This also meant he wished to obtain a precise account of what had happened in Germany during *Kristallnacht* and its aftermath. The persecution of the Jews did not stop after that tragic night, but was repeated day after day. The Nazis paid little heed to protests abroad.

In Montreal the Nazis in the Arcand groups did not remain passive. In 1938 they organized rallies in two large municipally owned venues—the Atwater and St. James Markets. The city administration had rented them these spaces despite vocal opposition. The mayor, Camilien Houde,[192] maintained that the Arcand gang had the right to assembly and police protection.

At one such meeting, in the hall of the St. James Market, I was one of the many people in attendance. In those days the R.C.M.P. had already started to keep an eye on the Nazis in Quebec, and took notes on the speeches delivered at their meetings. Arcand, therefore, endeavoured to make his meetings sound "patriotic" so that he would not be regarded as the agent of a foreign government.

The meeting opened with the national anthems, *O Canada*, and *God Save the King*. The hall was packed. A large number of policemen were on hand to maintain order. It was rumoured that the communists were planning to break up the meeting.

After a few short introductory speeches came the main speaker, Adrien Arcand. He was greeted by thunderous applause and the Hitler salute. On this occasion Arcand began by warning that the Jews wanted to impose a bloody war on the Christian world. He asked the audience: "Do you want to go to war and spill your blood for the sake of the Jews?"

"No! No!" came cries from all directions.

"Jewish agents are conspiring in Ottawa, Washington, and London to wage a war against the Germans who want to save Europe from Communism," Arcand shouted.

During such passionate anti-Jewish demonstrations, the police would remove from the hall a few young people suspected of intending to disrupt the proceedings.

A mass meeting at His Majesty's Theatre, Montreal, November 20, 1938, urged the Canadian government to help relieve the plight of German Jews. Chief Justice R.A. Greenshields acted as chairman. Other dignitaries included Brig.-gen. E. de B. Panet, Rabbi H. Abramovitz, Ven. Archdeacon Gower-Rees, Allan Bronfman, Col. A.A. Magree, W.A. Gifford and Louis Fitch, M.L.A. *Canadian Jewish Chronicle*, November 25, 1938.

On the Eve of the Second World War

The Fascist Victory in Spain. The Austrian *Anschluss*. The Munich Appeasement Agreement. The Stalin-Hitler Pact. The Dramatic Zionist Congress.

THE NEWS FROM EUROPE in the few years preceding the Second World War became increasingly dramatic and, in the final analysis, tragic. In 1936 Arab terrorism in Palestine escalated, causing grave concern in the Jewish communities of the United States and Canada. In Canada the distress was even greater because the British had adopted a negative attitude toward the Jewish *yishuv* in Palestine and tended to side with the Arabs. Canadian Zionists were unable to protest too loudly because Canada was part of the British Commonwealth. The Canadian Government, although sympathetic to the Zionist movement, was loyal to England, the motherland.

At that time the British were said to be worried about the possibility that Arabs in Iraq would sabotage England's interests in Iraqi oil wells, which were indispensable to the British navy. For this reason, the Colonial Office wanted to extricate itself from its commitments under the Balfour Declaration. However, the Jewish *yishuv* was sufficiently fortified and organized to be able to retain its hold on the foundations laid by the pioneer *chalutzim* in all parts of Eretz Israel.

The news from Europe was frightening. Nazi persecutions were becoming increasingly ruthless. The Nuremberg Laws[193] stripped the German Jews of all their rights. There was a sense that no matter how terrible the situation for the Jews in Germany had become, it would only get worse. The Nazis had already begun to speak of annihilating the Jewish race, including those who were only half or one-quarter Jewish.

In Spain a civil war was raging between the democratic loyalists and fascist rebels. All signs pointed to a fascist victory, which would mean the strengthening of the Berlin-Rome Axis. The danger for the Jewish future became critical. The enemies of world Jewry were acquiring an even greater appetite for world domination. The western powers became frightened. Until now, they had been under the illusion that the Nazis did not pose a threat. Hitler would be content with his battle against the Jews and communism.

In western countries like England, the United States, and even France, there were groups who claimed that the Germans had been entitled to certain concessions, and were now trying to use force where peaceful diplomacy had failed. When the Nazis invaded and occupied Austria in 1938, these groups responded: Why not? The Germans and the Austrians belong to the same race. Why should they not unite? Not so terrible! In London and Paris the government leaders, Prime Minister Neville Chamberlain and Prime Minister Daladier, barely even grimaced. They swallowed it.

When the Germans began to make noises about annexing the Sudetenland of Czechoslovakia, these same people said: "The Germans want to reclaim their own property. Germans live in the Sudetenland. Not such a terrible crime."

Chamberlain and Daladier went to meet Hitler for the purpose of reaching an understanding. He was given a free hand in the Sudetenland, but no more! He was not to make any further attempts to extend the borders of the Third Reich. When Chamberlain returned home after the appeasement pact with Hitler, he said he was very pleased that he had rescued peace. Peace, he announced, was now secure in our time.

But Hitler persevered. He demanded, and soon received, Memel, a former German port, which after World War I was annexed by Lithuania. Then he demanded the Danzig corridor, which belonged to Poland. By the beginning of 1939 it became clear to the leaders in London and Paris that the Munich Agreement had been a mistake, that Hitler's appetite for further expansion had not been sated. So they hurried to Moscow to attempt to conclude a treaty with Stalin to hold the Nazis in check.

However, it was already too late. Stalin had already dismissed his able foreign minister, Maxim Litvinoff, the Soviet representative in the League of Nations and ambassador to Washington, and replaced him with Molotov. And Stalin had done so because he had entered into negotiations with the Nazis in Berlin. The Jew Litvinoff was unsuitable for such negotiations. The world was stunned when it learned that Molotov and Ribbentrop, the Nazi foreign minister, had signed a non-aggression pact aimed at the western Allies.

This turn of events was especially tragic for the Jews who had believed that the communists and the Nazis were sworn enemies who would never negotiate with one another. Many Jews, despite their ideological opposition to communism, were still somewhat sympathetic to the Soviets because of their hatred of the Nazis. For these Jews the Stalin-Hitler Pact was a profound disappointment. It heightened the danger for world Jewry.

At the end of the summer of 1939 a Zionist congress, one of the most dramatic and disheartening congresses, took place in Geneva. That year England had prohibited Jewish immigration to Palestine, and the Second World War erupted. At the close of the congress, Weitzmann[194] said goodbye to the delegates from Poland with the words: "Who knows whether we shall ever see each other again." Delegates had trouble getting home, for Europe was already in a state of war. On August 31 the German armies invaded Poland.

In England, and here in Canada, as soon as the Second World War began, Zionist circles offered the British whatever assistance they could, including special Jewish military units to fight the Nazis and protect Palestine from external enemies.

Montreal, 1942.
(Left to right) Medres son Abe, son-in-law Irvine Glass, both in
the RCAF. the author, and son Phil, in the uniform of the Canadian Army.
Photo courtesy of Phil Madras

Canada's Role in the Second World War

Canadian Pilots in England during the Blitzkrieg. Jewish Pilots Who
Distinguished Themselves. Jewish Soldiers in the Canadian Army.

CANADA PLAYED an important role in World War II, especially in the period
before the entry of the United States into the war. Many people believed that
England would not have survived the frightening days of the Blitzkrieg had
the Canadian air force not come to its aid against Hitler's powerful Luftwaffe,
which reduced a number of major urban centres to rubble. The Germans had
triggered the war on September 1, 1939, when their army invaded Poland. Before
long, Polish resistance had crumbled. By virtue of the treaty concluded between
the Nazis and the Soviets, Poland was divided between them. The Nazis ceded
the eastern part of Poland, which included Polesia and Byelorussia, to the Soviets.

The Jews in Nazi-occupied Poland realized immediately that they were
living in death's shadow. The Nazis forced the Polish Jews into ghettos created
in several cities and towns. The largest ghetto was in Warsaw, the former hub
of Jewish cultural and social activity, where over 400,000 Jews were crowded
into a small area. Those who were healthy and able to work were sent as slave
labour for German industries. A campaign of terror was unleashed on the
Jews in the ghettos. The weakest, including women and children, were selected
to be sent to death camps, such as Auschwitz and Maidanek, where they were
murdered.

After the Nazi army had subjugated Poland, the Nazi Luftwaffe set its
sights on England. It now seemed that England was in grave danger, and
everyone wondered whether it would be able to endure. Winston Churchill
promised that England would fight to the last drop of blood.

In the earliest days of the war, Canada took the position that if England
was at war, Canada was also at war, and the decision was made to send
substantial aid as quickly as possible. The most effective assistance Canada
could give the motherland was a strong air force, capable of fighting the Nazi
Luftwaffe. Volunteers were immediately recruited to train as pilots, a profession
little known in Canada prior to that time.

Young Jews were among the first to volunteer for the armed forces, most of them enlisting in the air force. Within a short time Jewish youth appeared in the streets in uniform. Many of them, having distinguished themselves in the air force training schools, became officers.

As soon as war was declared, the attitude to Arcand's anti-Semitic gangs changed completely. The leaders and active members of this movement were interned as enemies of the country, among them Camilien Houde, the mayor of Montreal.

From time to time Mayor Houde had exhibited pro-fascist tendencies. At the beginning of the war there were people in the Province of Quebec who opposed Canada's participation. In Montreal demonstrations were organized against conscription. Protesters carried anti-Jewish placards claiming that the war was being waged on behalf of the Jews. Mayor Houde sided with those who protested against Canadian participation in the war, and exhorted French Canadians to refuse to enlist in the Canadian army. For this he was interned under the new security legislation hastily enacted by Parliament.

During the first few months of the war, the Nazi army operated only in Poland. The commonly held belief was that the Nazis were afraid to cross the Maginot Line into France. This extremely costly system of heavy fortifications was built to protect France. However, in the spring of 1940, the Nazi army invaded France through Belgium, completely avoiding the Maginot Line. The French army proved to be very weak, the French surrendered, and the Nazis occupied Paris and most of France. They allowed Marshall Pétain to control part of southern France, with Vichy as its capital.

At that time, Allied morale was very low. England's future looked very bleak. People were afraid that if England were defeated in the Blitzkrieg, the hand of Hitler would reach everywhere, even across the Atlantic.

In Washington, President Roosevelt promised that if Hitler's forces attempted to invade Canada, the United States would immediately enter the war. Although this was reassuring to Canada, apprehension persisted. This fear abated somewhat when it was reported that Canadian pilots were shooting down Nazi airplanes.

Each day during the Blitzkrieg, Canadian newspapers published lists of Canadian pilots who had downed Nazi warplanes. Very often one came across the names of Jewish boys from Montreal, Toronto, Winnipeg, and other places. These were the first North American Jews to have the opportunity to take revenge against the Nazis for the spilling of Jewish blood. Among the most distinguished heroes in the Royal Canadian Air Force were Jewish pilots.

The courageous Montreal fighter pilot Sydney Shulemson received much attention. He won the highest distinction in the RCAF for shooting down a large number of Nazi warplanes. A second Jewish flyer to be honoured with the highest medal for heroism was Irving Bodnoff of Ottawa. He was one of the pilots who noticed a Nazi submarine in the Atlantic and sank it.

Canada also organized a strong army which made a significant contribution during the battles on the northern European fronts.

Phillip Madras, 1942

Jews in the Canadian War Effort

The War Efforts Committees of the Canadian Jewish Congress.
Jewish Heroes in the Air Force. Jewish Soldiers in the Land Army.
Jewish Colonels in the Montreal Area.

WITH THE OUTBREAK of war in the fall of 1939, the Canadian Jewish Congress took immediate steps to organize all of Canadian Jewry for the war effort. Jewish communities all over the country were prepared to do their utmost to support the total war against the Nazis who had proclaimed themselves the mortal enemies of the Jewish people.

The Jewish Congress took the position that Canadian Jews had a greater obligation than other citizens of this country to contribute to the war effort. All sectors of the Jewish population were prepared to accept this obligation and demonstrated their willingness to do whatever was in their power to support the government's policy of total war.

Before the war Jews had thought they would be left to contend with the Nazis on their own. In their propaganda the Nazis and their supporters claimed they were not enemies of Canada, England, or France, but that their objective was solely to combat international Jewry and communism. Many non-Jews believed that if the Nazis started a war, the conflict would be limited to Eastern Europe, against the Soviet Union, and not the West. Therefore the Western powers were neither psychologically nor physically prepared for war against Hitler and his cohorts, who for years had been working around the clock to build a gigantic war machine with which to conquer the entire world.

The Canadian government gladly accepted the offer of the Canadian Jewish Congress to coordinate the activities of all the various Jewish communities for the war effort. To this end the Congress created a national Jewish War Efforts Committee.[195]

Jewish communities throughout the country became intensely active in every aspect of the total war against the Nazis, including the campaign to recruit volunteers for the Canadian armed forces. To raise the huge sums of money required for its costly war program, the government issued Victory Bonds. The Jewish community helped considerably in the sale of these bonds.

The government invested all its resources in the conduct of a total war for which it was ill-prepared. Almost everything had to be built from scratch. An air force had to be created overnight and military bases constructed all over the country. Once these camps were built, the Jewish Congress offered to help equip them with suitable furniture, especially those for use by officers. Samuel Bronfman, the president of the Canadian Jewish Congress, was at the forefront of all this activity. Mrs. Bronfman was in charge of recruiting Jewish women for the Red Cross, a contribution which was widely recognized.

In England Jewish communities also established special war efforts committees to support the total war against the Nazis. The dispute between the Zionist leaders and the British Colonial Office over England's Palestine policy was temporarily postponed. In 1939 England had further restricted Jewish immigration to Palestine. Zionist leaders were outraged, but with the outbreak of war they offered to create a special Jewish Legion to fight the Nazis, and England gratefully accepted.

Before the United States entered the war, American Jewish leaders applauded the efforts of Canadian Jews who had the opportunity of participating directly in the total war against Nazism. Many young American Jews enlisted in the Canadian armed forces, mainly in the RCAF. Certain political groups in the United States were advocating that America isolate itself from the problems of Europe and remain neutral in its dealings with both sides. Although President Roosevelt did not share the view of these isolationists, he was in no hurry to lead the United States to war—until the attack on Pearl Harbour. Before this event, Canada was the only country on the American continent to participate in the war against the Nazis. In the first months after war was declared, many young Jews donned Canadian military uniforms. For the most part, Jewish boys enlisted in the air force to become pilots or navigators. This service required a certain amount of training and skill. Young men who exhibited special ability in training school became commissioned officers.

Glowing reports were received about the Jewish flyers sent to England to fight the German Luftwaffe in the frightening days of the Blitzkrieg. Their names often appeared in the lists of heroes who had shot down Nazi airplanes. Naturally the parents of these brave pilots had reason to be proud, receiving congratulations from all quarters. Of course there were also casualties and parents who lost their sons somewhere over England, Belgium, or France.

Many young Jewish men also served in the army. In the Montreal area there were two well-known Jewish colonels, Colonel Joseph Echenberg, in charge of the ordinance depot in Longueuil, and Colonel Phillip Abbey, the commander of the large military base in Farnham. As a representative of the *Keneder Adler*, I often had the opportunity to visit the army bases and speak with the Jewish colonels about the Jewish soldiers under their command and in the Canadian army in general.

Colonel Echenberg came from a family of merchants in Sherbrooke, Quebec. In peacetime he had been involved in business and active in community affairs. Colonel Abbey was also a businessman and prominent participant in the philanthropic institutions of the Montreal Jewish Community. In the army he commanded an artillery regiment. Every time I spoke to him he would emphasize the uniqueness of this war. Jews were not being called upon to fight their fellow Jews. "We can be sure," he said, "that there are no Jewish soldiers on the Nazi side."

Colonel Abbey once invited me to a meal in the officers' mess at the Farnham base. There he introduced me to a number of officers, some of whom were Jews. One of the non-Jewish officers engaged me in conversation. He informed me that in his unit there were a few Jewish soldiers who, although all good boys, shared one fault—they had no patience. They were all in a hurry to cross the ocean and fight the Nazis. But in a war it was useless to rush. Proper training was essential.

There were even more Jewish soldiers under Colonel Echenberg's command. Apparently Jews were better suited for ordinance work, especially young men who had worked in offices or stores. During one of our discussions Colonel Echenberg stressed the idea that if—heaven forbid—the war were lost, there would be no little corner of the world where Jews would be welcome. Other nations would be allowed to live, some, perhaps, as slaves to the Nazis, but not the Jews. For them it would be the end.

This opinion was shared by many Jewish soldiers with whom I had the opportunity to speak in those days. The Canadian Jewish Congress set up a special committee responsible for the well-being of the Jewish servicemen. Moshe Meyerson, K.C., an active member of this committee, used to drive to the military base in Huntington where basic training took place. I often accompanied him and there met young Jewish men happy to be serving in the Canadian army. Indeed, many of them were impatient to leave Canada. They thought they had already received enough training to be in Europe and closer to the action. They considered theirs a twofold mission, to fight against the Nazis first as Canadian citizens, and secondly as Jews.

Lieut.-Col. Phillip Abbey, Commanding Officer, 2nd Field Brigade,
Royal Canadian Artillery. Medres went to interview him, and other Jewish officers,
at Camp Farnahm, Quebec in 1941.

Canadian Soldiers in the Role of Liberators

The First Canadian Army Drives the Germans out of Belgium and Holland.
How Canadian Jewish Soldiers Celebrated Chanukah with Rescued
Jewish Children.

IN THE FALL of 1944 it became clear that the powerful German army had lost its momentum. The Allies were gaining the upper hand on all fronts. The Americans had repelled the Germans in France, the Soviets had beaten them soundly in the Ukraine, and Rommel's army was stranded in Africa. To the Canadians fell the task of liberating Holland and Belgium.

The Canadian First Army had pierced through Nazi lines in Belgium and was advancing. In Canada we were proud to hear reports that our army had dealt the Nazis a decisive blow despite strong resistance. Although the Nazis had inflicted heavy losses, Canadian soldiers were successful in defeating them and proceeded to liberate one city after another.

At the time my wife and I were very moved upon reading a letter from our son, Fayvl,[196] who was with the Canadian army in Belgium and Holland. In this letter, which I printed in the *Keneder Adler*, he described how in one Dutch city,[197] the Canadian Jewish soldiers organized a Chanukah party for the local Jewish children. To accomplish this, they had to find the children and assemble them in the synagogue which had been locked up and abandoned. The synagogue needed to be repaired, cleaned, and made to look festive. Non-Jewish soldiers helped out in this work.

Rabbi Samuel Cass, one of the Jewish chaplains in the Canadian armed forces, was in charge of the Chanukah celebration. Whenever the Canadian army entered a Belgian or Dutch town or city, Rabbi Cass took it upon himself to find any surviving Jews, and bring them the news of the liberation. Jewish soldiers helped him find these liberated Jews in Antwerp, Amsterdam, Breda, Hilversum, Turnhout, and other places.[198] The Jews they discovered were given the means, with the assistance of the Canadian army, to celebrate their liberation.

Part of my son's letter is worth reproducing here. He recounts:

I came into the synagogue at 2:30 p.m. It was painful to see how the interior of the synagogue looked. We saw signs of the desecration committed by the Nazis who had destroyed whatever was connected with the synagogue. They had even torn up and broken all the pews. All that remained were four empty walls, a roof full of holes, and a damp and rotting floor. Nothing here resembled a synagogue. It looked more like an old, abandoned warehouse. Yet civilians, as well as servicemen, came here to pray.

The celebration was attended by servicemen from the Canadian army, as well as from the British and Polish armies, along with a few civilians, which made quite a sizeable congregation. Rabbi Cass gave a talk about Chanukah. Drawing a parallel between the conditions today and those in the days of the Maccabees, he said: "We have come back today to this house of God, sacked and plundered by the tyrannical enemy, the enemy we routed. We have returned to light the Chanukah candles. The same happened in the days of Judah the Maccabee, when they lit the oil lamp which the enemy of those days had desecrated ... we are repeating history."

After the celebration in the synagogue, we were invited to a private home. There a party had been prepared for small children who were unable to come to the synagogue. In the house were ten children and a few adults. The table had been set especially for the children, each of whom received packages of chocolate and candies prepared by Rabbi Cass and "the boys". We blessed and lit the Chanukah candles for the children, who, needless to say, were delighted. The adults were also exceptionally moved. This was the first time in several years that they had celebrated the holiday of Chanukah.

The tragic stories the Dutch Jews tell are similar to those we heard from the Jews of Belgium. The only difference is that the Jewish communities in Holland are proportionately smaller than those in Belgium. The Dutch Jews also had to endure several years of Nazi occupation. But one fact must be pointed out here. At the Chanukah celebration in the private house there was a Christian woman, a nurse. She had hidden seven Jewish children between the ages of two and seven. She had risked her life to hide these children from the Nazi murderers. One of the children is now a boy of four. No one knows where he comes from and what his name is. In the meantime, they call him Joseph ... All seven children rescued by the nurse were at the Chanukah party and together with them we celebrated the holiday of freedom. This celebration we will always remember.

This letter reflects the condition of the Jews of Europe immediately after the liberation. It also provides an illustration of the important role the Canadian army played in the great victory against the armies of Hitler who had aspired to conquer the world.

Liberated Jewish children celebrate Chanukah in Belgium.
The party was organized by Capt. Samuel Cass, Jewish chaplain
with the First Canadian Army.
Canadian Army Photo.
Canadian Jewish Congress National Archives

When Mikhoels and Feffer Visited Montreal

A Delegation from the Moscow Jewish Anti-Fascist Committee Comes to Montreal. A "Free" Conversation with Itzik Feffer in a St. Catherine Street Cafeteria.

WHEN THE SOVIETS entered the war, the general mood changed dramatically. Earlier, people had resented the Soviet government for having concluded the Non-Aggression Pact with the Nazis and, for this reason, considered the communists to be enemies. When Hitler's army invaded the Soviet Union, the anger dissipated and the Stalin regime became an ally and partner in the war against the Nazis. America poured huge amounts into this partnership in the form of Lend-Lease relief.[199]

With the Red Army now on the side of the Allies, there was hope that the Nazis would soon be defeated and the Jews liberated from Hitler's "fortress Europe". In those days many thought the Soviets were going to change their foreign policy and establish good relations with the democratic countries. Many Jews believed the iron curtain separating Soviet Jews from the Jews of other countries would be lifted.

This belief was strengthened when the Jewish Anti-Fascist Committee[200] of Moscow sent a delegation of two prominent Soviet Jews to meet with Jews in the United States and Canada. The delegation consisted of the famous actor S. Mikhoels[201] and the poet Itzik Feffer,[202] then a colonel in the Red Army.

Mikhoels and Feffer were warmly received in the cities they visited. They were the guests of the Soviet ambassador in Ottawa where a few representatives of the press were invited to a reception in a room at the Chateau Laurier. From Ottawa they came to Montreal[203] to address a rally at the Forum. First Mikhoels delivered a rousing speech which took the crowd by storm. He repeated the slogan "Death to Fascism", emphasizing that the fight against fascism united Jews all over the world. Then Itzik Feffer embarked on a bitter polemic. Speaking at length, he criticized those who fought against the communists. What he had to say was not of much interest to the majority in the audience, composed of all sectors of the Jewish population. Many people left the hall before he had finished speaking.

On the second day of their two-day visit to Montreal there was a reception at City Hall. When the official part of the program was over, Feffer approached me and said, "I understand you are from the *Keneder Adler*. I would like to ask you a favour."

"I will do whatever I can for you," I replied.

"Please, get me out of here. Even for an hour ... Do you understand?"

I understood. I let him out through a side exit. He asked to be taken to a self-service cafeteria. By taxi we drove to a cafeteria on St. Catherine street near Peel.

After we had helped ourselves to coffee and something to eat, he said, "Many newspaper people have been asking me questions. I had to give them answers. Now, please, let me ask you: What do Canadian Jews think of the Jewish Anti-Fascist Committee in the Soviet Union?"

"To the extent that the Committee is fighting against fascism," I answered, "this is very good. But, does it have any other purpose, in particular to strengthen secular Jewish cultural life?"

He replied that at present there was no task more important for Jews than the struggle against fascism. All efforts must be focussed on this struggle.

I agreed that the struggle against fascism, especially against Nazism, was now of prime importance. "But," I said, "this is no longer uniquely a Jewish cause. In addition to this struggle, Jews have other national responsibilities shared by Jewish communities everywhere, including those in Eastern Europe. We believe that you and Mikhoels are directly, or indirectly, the representatives of the Soviet Jews in this great undertaking."

He told me that although he was a Marxist, he had a positive attitude to secular Jewish culture. He could say the same about a number of his colleagues on the anti-Fascist committee.

I asked him, if such was the case, whether he or his colleagues would establish Jewish schools to teach secular Jewish culture and socialist Zionism, like the schools created by secular Jews in America and Canada. After thinking for a while, he responded, "The struggle against fascism is paramount ..." Thus ended our conversation.

Riding in the back of a taxi to the Bucharest Restaurant, where he and Mikhoels were scheduled to be the guests of honour at a luncheon, we said nothing more about secular Jewish culture or the struggle against fascism. Feffer expressed regret that we had talked too much in the cafeteria ... People would be waiting … He looked preoccupied, worried. He complained that he had hardly slept. His stomach was bothering him. I was sorry that I had taken him out at all. To me he now looked like a sensitive Jewish poet, proud of his Jewish heritage but struggling with Marxism, which would not allow him to be free.

I saw him as a Jew oppressed by Marxism.

November 5, 1944. The Canadian Federation of Russian Jews transfers a $10,000 shipment of new clothing to the Bobruisk region of the Soviet Union. Seated are (left to right) Mr. Gorelik, J. Glassman, Mrs. N. Resnik, S. Lapitsky, Mrs. M. Crystal, and Joseph Yass. Standing are Louis Hyman, A. Ostrovsky, A. Fleisher, I. Medres, Milton Kelin, M. Miller, J. Golfman, and S. Temkin. *Canadian Jewish Chronicle*, November 17, 1944.

The First Jewish War Immigrants

A Group of Eighty Scholars Who Came from Japan. Young German Jews Who Were
Brought from England. Refugees Who Were Saved in Portugal.

JEWISH IMMIGRANTS who succeeded in escaping Hitler's "fortress Europe"
began trickling into Canada even before the war was over. In 1941 a group of
scholars arrived, among them heads of yeshivas and their students. This group
had come through Japan.

Other groups arrived, having crossed Siberia to reach Tokyo or Shanghai.
Some Jews who came to Canada from Portugal had been smuggled across the
French border with the assistance of the anti-Nazi underground. These immigrants were Polish citizens for whom the Polish government in exile had
obtained visas.

It was far more difficult to convince the government in Ottawa to allow
these refugees into Canada. The government was faced with strong opposition
to immigration. Nevertheless, from time to time, a group of stateless Jewish
victims of Nazi terror was granted permission to enter Canada on humanitarian grounds.

With regard to the group of scholars from Japan, extensive lobbying was
conducted in Ottawa on their behalf. A large delegation went to see the
immigration minister to appeal to him to reverse an earlier negative ruling.
Participating in this delegation were Saul Hayes[204] and M. Garber[205] of the
Canadian Jewish Congress, H. Wolofsky,[206] Honourary President of the
Federation of Polish Jews, and Peter Bercovitch, [207] Member of Parliament.
The delegation succeeded in gaining admission for the eighty scholars and
fifty other Jews who had relatives in Canada.

When the members of this group arrived in Montreal, they were welcomed
with open arms and given the assistance required to enable them to pursue
their religious studies here in Canada. No one imagined at that time that this
group would spawn two large yeshivas in Montreal, the Lubavitch yeshiva,
Tomchei Tmimim, and the Merkaz HaTorah Yeshiva, which would significantly

enrich Jewish religious life and Jewish education.

Another interesting group of Jewish refugees was composed of young German and Austrian Jews transported to Canada from England as prisoners of war. Although it was well known that they did not support the governments of their countries of origin, because of legal technicalities they had to be detained as enemy aliens.

The Canadian government brought them here to assist England where food was insufficient for so many prisoners of war. England also lacked the manpower to guard the detainees. Therefore the Canadian government offered to take a certain number and intern them for the duration of the war.

This group was housed in a camp not far from Montreal, on Ile-aux-Noix in the Richelieu River.[208] The government informed the Canadian Jewish Congress of their arrival, and allowed the Congress to treat them not as "enemies", but as fellow Jews.

The Canadian Jewish Congress and the ORT[209] organization immediately set to work to help this group of young people. The ORT brought machinery to teach them various skills required at the time in the munitions industry. An ORT delegation drove to Ottawa to appeal to the federal government to allow a technical school to be established at the Ile-aux-Noix camp. In that delegation were Lord Marley[210] of England and Dr. D. Lvovich,[211] both leaders of the world ORT organization, as well as Saul Hayes of the Canadian Jewish Congress.

At this time ORT was very active in Montreal. Under the direction of Vladimir Grossman, a well-known journalist and community activist, a technical school organized by ORT gave specialized instruction in the metal trades required by the war industry. Louis Fitch was then the president of ORT.

While negotiations were underway with the federal authorities to change their status from enemy alien, the young detainees eagerly learned new skills. Finally, the government acknowledged that they were not enemies, but allies of a democratic Canada and a democratic England, and they were released from the internment camps.

As I have mentioned, there were also immigrants who came from Portugal. Men, women, and children had miraculously escaped from France through the Pyrenees into Portugal where they were protected from the Nazis. Upon their arrival, they were taken under the wing of the Jewish Immigrant Aid

Society. The Jewish community happily welcomed these refugees who told fantastic tales of their deliverance. They owed their lives to the heroes of the anti-Nazi underground in France.

They recounted how Christian families had risked their own lives to hide Jewish women and children from the Nazis. Catholic priests and nuns in French towns hid them in churches until the heroes of the Resistance arrived. During the day they lay hidden in churches, cellars, or barns, and at night they climbed through secret mountain passes, with young children in their arms, until they came to the Portuguese border. Even the children, born in France and speaking only French, understood why they had to hide by day and run by night. They knew their lives were in danger because they were "Israelites".

Those little refugees of long ago are today valuable citizens of Canada.

Office of the Canadian Jewish Congress and War Efforts Committee,
Holland Building (Ste. Catherine corner Peel), Montreal, 1941.
In the second row on the right is Anne Medres, daughter of Israel Medres,
sitting next to Sylvia Salzman who would later become Medres' daughter-in-law.
Courtesy of Sylvia Madras

When the Cataclysm Ended

The Total Defeat of the Nazis. Liberated Europe. Exchange of Jewish Delegations.
The Historic Nuremberg Trials.

IT WAS A MOMENTOUS DAY when the Nazis surrendered on May 7, 1945. They
had waged a total war, and suffered a total defeat. Although Jews the world
over welcomed this defeat with jubilation, their happiness was tinged with
sorrow. They knew the Nazis had annihilated six million European Jews. It
was the greatest catastrophe in Jewish history.

The Canadian Jewish Congress became active at once in rescuing the survivors of various European concentration camps whom the Nazis had not
succeeded in murdering. Providing whatever assistance it could, the Congress
collaborated with the American Joint Distribution Committee (the Joint)[212]
in the United States in this relief work.

In the beginning we thought the liberated Jews would soon be able to
settle safely in Palestine and elsewhere. Unfortunately, it turned out quite
differently. The British authorities refused to allow them into Palestine, and
other countries imposed severe restrictions on immigration. The White Paper,
in force since 1939, had closed the gates of Palestine to Jewish immigration.
In the first few years after the war a battle raged between the Zionists and the
British Colonial Office over this prohibition which remained in effect until
the English withdrew from Palestine.

The liberated Jews were forced to remain in camps for a prolonged period
of time. They lived there in freedom, of course, but not knowing where their
permanent home would be. They were called Displaced Persons or D. P.s –
rootless and stateless people who belonged nowhere.

The Jewish rescue organizations of North America and England immediately undertook to assist the Jews in the D.P. camps. The United Refugee Relief
Committee of the Canadian Jewish Congress collaborated closely with the
American Joint, which played a leading role. The Joint had established offices
in the various parts of Europe where the camps were located to care for the

refugees and facilitate their recovery from the horrific ordeal they had suffered at the hands of the Nazis.

One of the directors of the Joint in those days was Lavy Becker of Montreal. He was in charge of the Joint's relief work in the American zone. In a report issued in April 1946 and published in the press, he noted that of the 80,000 Jews then in Germany, about 60,000 were under his supervision. A majority of them, about 35,000, were housed in camps. Some were in *Hakhshara* camps, where they were being trained for agricultural work in Palestine, and the rest had been placed in civilian homes. They were all receiving meagre food rations from UNRRA, the United Nations Relief and Rehabilitation Administration, barely enough to keep body and soul together. The Joint provided them with necessary additional food, and tended to their social, cultural, and religious needs.

The Jews in the German camps wanted very much to go to Palestine, but the White Paper admitted only a small number each month. The immigration certificates were given to children who for the most part were already young adults. Some had fought as partisans in the underground struggle against the Nazis, Mr. Becker reported.

When Mr. Becker completed his duties in Europe and returned to Montreal he was very involved in the rescue activities of the Canadian Jewish Congress, and to this day remains an important figure in the leadership of Congress.

As soon as Europe was freed from the Nazi occupation, the Canadian Jewish Congress decided to establish ties with all the liberated Jewish communities. To this end, it sent a delegation to Poland to make contact with Polish Jews and find out what could be done to help them. The delegation consisted of H. M. Caiserman,[213] general secretary of the Congress, and Samuel Lipschitz,[214] a representative of the United Jewish People's Order.[215] Since Poland was under a communist regime, Congress deemed it appropriate for Mr. Caiserman to be accompanied by a person who was connected with the left-wing movement.

The Jews in Poland gave the Canadian Jewish Congress delegation a warm reception. Consequently, a delegation of Polish Jews, led by the well-known community activist and Zionist leader Dr. Emil Sommerstein,[216] visited Canada soon afterward. This large delegation included representatives of all the various Jewish organizations in Poland at the time. The Canadian Jewish Congress and the Association of Polish Jews hosted them with enthusiasm. In fact, they were welcomed by all the Jews of Canada for whom they symbolized the surviving remnant of European Jewry. They also represented the Jewish heroes who had fought the Nazis in the ghettos and forests of Poland as members of the anti-Nazi underground.

The patriarchal appearance of Dr. Emil Sommerstein, who until 1939 was a member of the Polish *Sejm*, made a forceful impression. He was one of the principal speakers at a rally in His Majesty's Theatre under the chairmanship of Dr. Michael Garber.[217] In the delegation was a young woman of twenty-five named Chaya Grossman who described her experiences in the Warsaw ghetto uprising against the Nazis in 1943. The delegation also visited Toronto, where the Jewish community gave them a heartfelt reception.

Immediately after the end of the war it appeared as though the friendship between East and West would certainly continue. We believed that just as people were able to die together in the war against Nazism, they would also be able to live together. There had emerged a dynamic movement called Aid to Russia, which attracted Jews of various affiliations and convictions. They collected used clothing and sent it to people in Russia regardless of race or religion.

The friendship with the Soviets was based, above all, on gratitude to the Red Army, which had made tremendous sacrifices in the struggle against Nazism. Initially the Red Army had suffered serious setbacks, losing one battle after another while the Nazis conquered much of European Russia. They besieged Leningrad, destroyed other urban centres, and were approaching the gates of Moscow. The Red Army sustained heavy losses in both Kiev and Kharkov, two large cities in the Ukraine.

The first Soviet victory, which proved to be a decisive one, was at Stalingrad in 1943. It was a historic victory which dealt a fatal blow to the powerful German war machine. From then on, the Nazis were on the defensive. At the same time they were routed at Al Alamein, Egypt, where Rommel's army had been threatening the entire Middle East, including Eretz Israel.

The Nazi army suffered its final defeat near Berlin. When Hitler saw the Red Army closing in on him he took his own life, and his generals surrendered to the Allies. Nazi political and military leaders were quickly arrested and sent to Nuremberg to be tried in an international court by judges from the United States, the Soviet Union, France, and England.

The historic trial, which lasted a year, took place in the same city where ten years earlier the Nazis had enacted the racist Nuremberg laws against the Jews. It was only natural that Jews all over the world, who had been so distraught over the Nuremberg laws, would be more gratified than anyone else to see Nazis brought to justice. The majority of those found guilty were sentenced to the gallows. One of the most important Nazis, Wilhelm Goering,[218] poisoned himself in prison the night before he was to have been hanged. Among the two or three Nazi leaders who managed to escape was Adolph Eichmann. He succeeded in hiding in Argentina where he lived for a number of years. As is well known, he was captured by Jewish secret agents, who brought him to Israel in a very clever way. There he was tried by a Jewish court and sentenced to death. In the end, he shared the fate of the other Nazi ringleaders.

V. E. Day, May 8, 1945.
Celebrating the announcement of the surrender of German forces in Europe outside the office of the Canadian Jewish Congress, Ste. Catherine and Peel.
Courtesy of Sylvia Madras

Immigrant Tailors from the D.P. Camps[219]

The Situation of the Liberated Jews after the Defeat of Hitler. Freedom and
Homelessness. The Delegation to Bring Tailors from the D.P. Camps.

WHEN THE SECOND WORLD WAR had ended and the defeated German army
had surrendered, all the Jews imprisoned in Hitler's camps were automatically
liberated. Their joy at being free was boundless, but for a very long time they
remained homeless and isolated.

At first we expected the victorious nations to immediately open their doors
to the survivors and welcome them with open arms. But the reality was quite
different. They were forced to remain in the D.P. camps where they lived for
an extended period as refugees, as people without a country.

Jewish relief organizations in the United States and Canada made every
effort to find homes for the ill-fated refugees but no concrete results were
achieved. The Canadian government, like other Western governments, while
pretending to be very sympathetic to the Jewish survivors of Hitler's persecution, was in no hurry to open its doors. There were groups who protested
against admitting the refugees from Europe into the country on the ground
that this would result in unemployment for Canadian workers. They also
claimed that an influx of refugees would create a housing shortage and lead to
rent increases. The government opened the doors ever so slightly to allow in a
few carefully chosen immigrants.

At the time, the Canadian government was only accepting immigrants
required by industries for which there were no skilled workers in Canada. Just
as in the aftermath of World War I, following World War II there was large-
scale industrial expansion. Brand new industries were created, and existing
ones expanded. Some manufacturers made it known that they lacked
manpower for their factories.

The government allowed manufacturers to bring skilled labourers from
Europe if they met two conditions. First they had to demonstrate that they
were unable to find suitable workers in Canada. Secondly they had to show

that their Canadian employees did not object to bringing in workers from abroad.

In Montreal a movement was launched to take advantage of this opportunity and bring over more Jewish refugees from the D.P. camps in Germany and Austria. The initiative was taken by organized labour, with the International Ladies Garment Workers Union the first to become involved. To set this project in motion it was necessary for the union together with the Association of Manufacturers of Ladies' Garments to submit a joint petition to the government for permission to bring refugees from Europe with the tailoring skills urgently required by the industry.

Permission was granted, and in 1947 a delegation from the Canadian women's clothing industry travelled to Europe to find qualified tailors. Heading this delegation was Bernard Shane,[220] currently the vice-president of the International and treasurer of the Jewish Workers' Committee, which was also an active participant in this relief project. The task of the delegation was to examine the qualifications of the refugee tailors wishing to come to Canada.

This delegation brought 4,000 tailors to Canada, about 1,000 of them for the men's clothing industry. They were sent to Montreal, Toronto, and Winnipeg. The relief operation was an historic event. From the moment the refugee Jewish tailors arrived in Canada, they were cared for financially and otherwise by the Canadian Jewish Congress and the Jewish Immigrant Aid Society. The union ensured that they were provided with employment in the shops.

Mr. Bernard Shane talked to me about his experience in Germany during his 1947 visit, two years after the end of the war. He was one of the first Canadian civilians to visit Germany after the Nazis capitulated to the Allies. In Hanover, the first city he visited, he was confronted by the frightening sight of large buildings reduced to mountains of shattered brick. From under the heaps of rubble crept living people, dispirited creatures.

Face to face with such destruction and devastation, a Jewish spectator could not help experiencing mixed emotions. On the one hand, there was the desire for retribution. The Germans were now suffering for having supported Hitler. They were paying the price of a defeat they deserved. They, the members of Hitler's superior race, were now crawling like worms. On the other hand, they were still human beings! It was difficult watching people forced to live under such appalling conditions. Feelings of vindictiveness and empathy were intermingled.

Near Hanover was a notorious death camp where the Nazis brutally murdered their victims. Mr. Shane told me that near the camp he was shown mounds of earth which covered large mass graves. One was the grave of captured Russian soldiers, another a large grave of Poles. In the largest were buried Jews. Seeing the graves rekindled the desire for revenge.

In Frankfurt there were similar scenes. One part of the city remained intact, while another had been reduced to piles of brick, clay, and twisted pieces of iron. The Allies had bombed according to a set plan, sparing the train station and hotels so that the victorious Americans, British, and French would have a place to stay after the war.

These scenes of Germans living among the ruins were repeated in Stuttgart. Shadowy figures prowled the streets like hungry dogs in search of scraps of food.

In Vienna, the Austrian capital, then under the control of the Soviets, the large cooperative apartment complexes built by socialists and workers had been smashed to bits. The commercial streets somehow were left untouched.

The immigrants chosen from these cities, as well as from Salzburg, were brought to Canada by ship. Each immigrant was permitted to bring his wife and children. Altogether they were a sizeable group of people. This became evident once they arrived in Canada.

Similarly, refugee tailors were brought over for the men's clothing industry. In 1948 a delegation led by Max Federman, manager of the Toronto Fur Workers' Union, delivered 500 furriers. Mr. Morris Silcoff, vice-president of the Milliner's Union, led a delegation to the camps to find qualified millinery workers.

These refugees breathed new life into the Jewish community. They themselves were very happy to have come here, and in the shops they were welcomed with warmth and friendliness by their co-workers.

Among the refugees was a group which had arrived before the end of the war thanks to the assistance of the Jewish Workers' Committee. This committee had established close contact during the war with the anti-Nazi underground in Nazi-occupied Europe. The committee would send financial aid collected from the labour movement and anti-Nazi circles in the United States and Canada. Thanks to the influence wielded by the committee in government circles in Washington, it received visas for hundreds of Jewish, as well as non-Jewish, trade union and socialist leaders who had managed to hide from the Nazis. Several hundred settled in the United States and some in Canada. A few of those who came to Montreal now have important positions in the labour movement, and especially in the Jewish Workers' Committee.

Jewish DPs Welcome United Jewish Appeal delegation.
Canadian Jewish Chronicle, March 1, 1948.

The Difficult Road to Freedom

The Struggle for the Jewish Homeland in the First Few Years after the
Second World War. The Zionist Convention which Adopted the Dominion Plan.

WHEN WORLD WAR II was over and Nazism eradicated, Jews were the first to
breathe the fresh air of freedom. But the road to the full-fledged freedoms
they expected was far from smooth. Again it became necessary to resume the
struggle for Palestine in addition to finding new homes for liberated Jews
waiting in the so-called D.P. camps, the camps for Displaced Persons, the rootless refugees.

In the first few years after the war the question of the Land of Israel was
the prime preoccupation of the Jewish leadership in North America and
England. In 1946 the fighting in Palestine involving the Jews, the Arabs, and
the British intensified. This situation was exacerbated in 1947.

In June of 1946 the mandate authorities had arrested the entire executive
of the Jewish Agency[221] in order to break the Jewish opposition to the White
Paper limiting Jewish immigration to Palestine. The arrests of the Jewish
Agency leaders shocked the entire Jewish world. The British occupied the Jewish
Agency building, as well as the offices of the *Keren Kayemet*[222] and the *Keren
Hayesod*.[223] In Tel Aviv, British police raided the headquarters of the Hista-
drut[224] and the offices of the newspaper *Davar*, causing a great deal of damage.

Among the Jewish leaders arrested at that time and incarcerated in the
Latrun prison were Moshe Shertok (Sharett),[225] David Remez,[226] Dov Yosef,[227]
Yizhak Gruenbaum,[228] Aba Hushi[229] and the old Mizrahi leader, Rabbi Yehuda
Fishman.[230] Two eminent leaders of the Jewish Agency, David Ben-Gurion[231]
and Eliezer Kaplan,[232] were abroad at the time.

As I have already noted, the Jewish *yishuv* and the British were engaged in
a bitter struggle. But the Jews disagreed among themselves over the methods
to be employed in this struggle. The *Irgun*, the military arm of the Revisionists
(Herut),[233] resorted to terrorism. Members of this group would attack British
police stations and inflict extensive damage. But this only provoked the British

135

to take severe punitive measures against the *yishuv*. On the other hand, the *Haganah*[234] advocated self-restraint and warned against the use of violence. Dr. Weitzmann and other Zionist leaders also denounced the terrorist tactics of the *Irgun*, which had resulted in the British authorities sentencing four of its members to death for conducting a raid on a police station. All four were executed.

The struggle against the British mandate authorities was also conducted on the political front in the United States, Canada, and England, and took a very dramatic turn during the first few years after World War II. In Canada, Zionist leaders were not as actively involved in this struggle as their counterparts in the United States. The fact that Canada was part of the British Commonwealth could not be disregarded, and public opinion had to be taken into account. However, they did not conceal their bitter disappointment over the attitude of the mandate authorities toward Jewish settlement in Palestine.

The 28th Convention of the Canadian Zionist Organization took place at the beginning of 1946. Dissatisfaction with Britain's policies was emphatically expressed. At this convention there were lengthy discussions over what demands should be presented to England and the United Nations with regard to Eretz Israel. Various proposals were debated. One plan called for Eretz Israel to become a British dominion and a member of the Commonwealth. According to this plan, Eretz Israel would not be completely independent. Although the British government would not interfere in the internal affairs of the *yishuv*, it would retain responsibility for the security of Eretz Israel.

Another proposal was to place Palestine under a United Nations trusteeship. The Soviets supported this plan. Evidently they were interested in being involved in this trusteeship to gain a foothold in the Middle East. This plan, opposed by Weitzmann, was rejected for it suffered from the same shortcomings as the British mandate. Jews would not have full control over Palestine.

There remained the partition plan to divide Palestine into two states, a Jewish state and an Arab state. Although Weitzmann did not like this plan, he advocated its acceptance because there was no other solution. It would be better to have a small state that was independent than to be under a United Nations trusteeship or a dominion under England.

At the 28th Convention of Canadian Zionists, held in Toronto, a resolution was adopted in favour of the Dominion Plan in the absence of a better solution. The resolution also expressed the strong disappointment of Canadian Jews over England's attitude towards the Jewish *yishuv* in Eretz Israel. It emphasized the fact that Jews were fully confident that in proclaiming the Balfour Declaration, England had manifested a basically positive attitude to Jewish needs. Within a Dominion system opportunities would be created for the Zionist goal to be realized under England's supervision.

The Dominion Plan, however, did not find much support beyond Canada's borders. In the United States and within the United Nations pressure for an independent Jewish homeland intensified. It was an uphill battle. Again a commission was appointed—an American-British commission—to study the possibilities for Eretz Israel and balance the interests of Jews and Arabs. As a result, in November of 1947 the General Assembly of the United Nations adopted a resolution recognizing Jewish rights to an independent homeland in Palestine. At the 29th Convention of the Canadian Zionist Organization, which took place in Ottawa in 1948, the Canadian government was thanked profusely for its important contribution in the General Assembly which led to the creation of the State of Israel.

Chaim Weitzmann, Cartierville Airport, Montreal. In 1942 the future president of Israel visited Montreal.
Canadian Jewish Congress National Archives.

The Historic Day

When the Jewish State Was Proclaimed. The Impact on the Jewish Community in Canada. The Arab War against the State of Israel.

FRIDAY, MAY 14, 1948 was a day of celebration. A ceremony in Tel Aviv proclaimed an independent Jewish state. This holiday was celebrated in all the Jewish communities of the United States and Canada. For the first time in Jewish history of the last 2,000 years Jews had their own country. The day before the ceremony in the Tel Aviv Museum, the British announced their withdrawal from Palestine.

The British did not leave of their own accord. In the bitter struggle between the British administration and the Jewish *yishuv*, the British had been unable to control the flow of immigration. Jewish immigrants arrived on small battered ships, evading the British authorities both at sea and in the harbours. When refugees who were considered illegal immigrants were caught, they were interned on the island of Cyprus.

The anti-Zionist policy of the mandate authorities dated back to the 1930s. The Arabs had responded with a violent uprising to Zionist efforts to build a country in compliance with the Balfour Declaration. In order to protect itself, the *yishuv* organized armed forces against Arab terrorists. Most prominent among these fighting organizations were the Irgun, under the supervision of the Revisionists, and the Haganah, organized by the Labour parties. Both organizations provided strong opposition to the anti-Zionist policies of the British mandate authorities.

In 1939, the same year the Nazis began the Second World War, the British issued the White Paper to stop Jewish immigration to Palestine. This sparked a strong reaction in every Jewish community. The organized Zionists in Montreal sent sharp letters of protest to the British government in London. Labour Zionist groups made their objections known to the British Labour party. While certain of its leaders were sympathetic to Zionism, others, such as the Colonial Ministers Passfield[235] and Ernest Bevan,[236] caused profound disappointment. Passfield was an intellectual socialist, a theoretician, and political journalist. When he was appointed colonial minister, it was expected that he would act completely within the spirit of the Balfour Declaration. However, he went a long way to appease the Arabs at the expense of England's commitments to the Zionists.

When the war was over, there was a belief that the time had come to ask the victors to take concrete steps toward the creation of a Jewish homeland in Palestine. It took two years until a resolution was adopted in the United Nations in November 1947, giving the Jewish people the opportunity to create an independent Jewish homeland.

For Canadian Jews, it was especially gratifying to know that the Canadian government had made a significant contribution to the adoption of this resolution. Of all the member countries of the British Commonwealth, Canada had displayed the strongest will to help achieve Zionist objectives. This was largely thanks to the tireless efforts of the Canadian Jewish Congress and all the Zionist organizations affiliated with the United Zion Council. When the United Nations passed the resolution on Eretz Israel, it was a day of celebration for the Jewish communities of Canada.

The U.N., however, did nothing to help found the Jewish state. The Jews were left to do this on their own. This was accomplished on May 14, 1948 when the State of Israel was officially proclaimed. For the Jewish people, it was an historic day.

Rally, Montreal, May 16, 1948, celebrating the proclamation of the State of Israel.
Canadian Jewish Congress Naitonal Archives.

Canada and Israel

Political Zionism during World War II. The Biltmore Resolution of the American Zionists. The Negotiations with Regard to Eretz Israel in the United Nations.

THE CANADIAN GOVERNMENT had always displayed a sympathetic attitude toward Zionist objectives. Its friendship was manifest even in the difficult years when Zionists were forced to conduct a bitter campaign against the British Colonial Office. This positive attitude was evident both under the Conservatives as well as the Liberals.

Although in international affairs Canada always supported the motherland, when it came to Palestine and the demand for the creation of an independent Jewish State in Palestine after World War II, Canada sided with the United States rather than with England. Presumably this was due to the effort of the Zionist movement in Canada, which intensified in the 1930s and during the war years.

More than ever before, Canada displayed its sympathy to Zionism in 1947 when the United Nations was deliberating about Palestine and the Zionist Organization's request to create a Jewish State in Eretz Israel, then under the British mandate. While World War II was raging, Eretz Israel had received a large number of Jewish refugees. But many more refugees could have been absorbed had the British authorities not adopted a negative stance to Zionism in an attempt to placate the Arabs who vehemently opposed both the Balfour Declaration and Jewish immigration.

At the beginning of the 1940s the Zionist initiative was taken over entirely by the Zionist organization in the United States. American Zionists endorsed the position that as soon as the war was over they would demand an end to the British mandate and the creation of a Jewish state in Eretz Israel. This demand was formulated at an historic convention of American Zionists in 1942 in the Biltmore Hotel in New York. The resolution adopted there was known for a long time as the Biltmore Resolution.

In those days people believed that the United States would emerge from the war as the strongest power in the West. Even if the Germans were defeated, the British, weakened by the war, would not be able to balance Jewish and Arab interests. Because of their oil interests in the Middle East, the British were unable to deal fairly with Zionist aspirations.

At the end of the war, elections were held in England. The Conservatives lost, and the Labour Party came to power under Prime Minister Clement Atlee. Zionists, especially Labour Zionists, hoped that the attitude of the Colonial Office would improve. They believed that the socialists in the Labour Party would be more sympathetic to the Jews in Eretz Israel, and take into consideration both the terrible suffering of the Jewish people during the Second World War and the major role being played by Jewish socialists in the building of a new Jewish society in Eretz Israel.

However, once again came painful disappointments. The colonial minister in the Labour government, Ernest Bevan, categorically refused to rescind the White Paper of 1939 restricting Jewish immigration. Renewed friction developed between the *yishuv* in Eretz Israel and the British Colonial Office.

In 1947 the political efforts of the Jewish Agency became focused on the United Nations Organization where Jewish leaders presented their demand for a Jewish homeland in Palestine and an end to Jewish homelessness. The U.N. General Assembly received the representatives of the Jewish Agency at its session in May of 1947. All aspects of the Palestine problem were discussed. The Assembly appointed a special committee to study the entire problem of Palestine and the Arabs, and to make recommendations as to how to proceed.

A few months later, in early autumn, the eleven members of the committee filed a report recommending an end to the British mandate and the division of Palestine into two separate states, Jewish and Arab, with economic cooperation for the benefit of both peoples.

Canadian representatives in the U.N. then played a decisive role. The Arab states, and a few others, strongly opposed a Jewish state in Palestine. When the vote was taken at the end of November, a majority of the thirty-three member states, including Canada, voted in favour of a Jewish homeland. Among those countries abstaining was England. In this instance Canada followed the lead of Washington rather than London.

While the debate on Palestine was taking place in the United Nations, I happened to be in Ottawa visiting the office of the minister for external affairs, the Honourable Louis St. Laurent, who later became prime minister. I had been sent by the *Keneder Adler* to obtain a clear statement with regard to

Canada's position on the Jewish problem in Palestine. Maurice Hartt,[237] a Jewish Member of Parliament, accompanied me.

Louis St. Laurent's statement contained the following:

> I am happy that my government can make a contribution to the creation of a Jewish State in Palestine. This is the realization of a divine prophesy in our time. We know it will benefit both the Jewish and the Arab peoples. We extend our friendship to Jews and Arabs alike. We are confident that both peoples can live together in peace, just as here in Canada various races live in a spirit of harmony, tolerance and friendship.

Mr. St. Laurent and the present prime minister, Lester Pearson, then in the Department of External Affairs and Canada's representative at the United Nations, made many positive contributions toward the creation of the State of Israel.

The Impact of Israel

Relations between Zionists and Non-Zionists. Reports of Jewish Heroism.
Expansion of the Hebraist Movement. Problems of Zionism.

THE CREATION OF THE JEWISH STATE raised the prestige of the Jewish people
all over the world, including Canada. The impact of this historic event helped
to unite all sectors of the Jewish community. The differences between Zionists
and non-Zionists began to disappear. It appeared as though all Jews, without
exception, were very enthusiastic about every aspect of the new Jewish state.
They were prepared to assist in the development of the new country, particularly in the absorption of more immigrants, who were expected to stream
in from all over, including the United States and Canada.

A few weeks after the proclamation of the State, the news from Israel was
far from encouraging. Arab armies were waging a war against the young state
and threatening to drive all the Jews into the sea. But it was hoped that the
courageous Israeli army would be able to defend the Jewish state, and prevent
the Arabs from perpetrating another holocaust. And these hopes were realized.
The Arabs were caught off-guard by the strength and bravery of the Israeli
youth. The hastily organized Israeli army fought back and fought valiantly.
The Arab attack was also a challenge to Jewish youth in other countries. In
those days we heard about young American and Canadian Jews joining the
ranks of the Israeli army to help defend the young Jewish state.

Once Israel had won the war, Jewish prestige rose again. Jews were now
seen in a different light, as a people which had borne arms against its enemies
and fought with courage and heroism. This heroism was not new to Jews.
Only a few years earlier we had heard about Jewish heroism in the ghettos,
especially in Warsaw where the Nazis had suffered heavy casualties. Although
the Germans eventually destroyed the ghetto, killing tens of thousands of Jews,
they paid a heavy price. During the several days that they were forced to engage
in battle against the Jews of the ghetto, many German soldiers lost their lives.

Jewish heroism was also evident in the underground struggle against the
Nazis in various parts of occupied Europe. Many Jews, both men and women,

distinguished themselves in these underground campaigns. From Eretz Israel brave guerrilla fighters were sent to participate in acts of sabotage against the Nazis. At the risk of their lives, they were parachuted into German-occupied areas. An example of this type of hero was the young Hannah Szenes.[238] She was parachuted into Hungary where her mission was to find young Jews who could be smuggled out of Hitler's Europe and brought to Eretz Israel. She was captured and shot by the Nazis. Her name has remained a symbol of Jewish heroism and self-sacrificing idealism.

The tremendous courage displayed by the Jewish youth in Israel during the War of Independence earned the admiration of the entire world.

The influence of the State of Israel had an impact on all aspects of Jewish life, especially in the social and cultural spheres. Jewish diplomats symbolizing Jewish statehood and national independence began arriving. The first diplomat from Israel to Canada as the official representative of the Jewish state was Abraham Harman, today the Israeli ambassador to Washington. For Canadian Jews this was an historic occasion. After Harman, Michael Comay came to Ottawa as Israel's first ambassador to Canada.[239]

The attitude to Jewish education grew much more positive, and the Hebrew cultural movement gained more visibility and importance. The Hebrew organization *Keren Hatarbut* became a leading force in building a spiritual and cultural bridge linking the Jews of Canada to the State of Israel. Under the leadership of Zalman Gordon, national president, this organization gave new impetus to Hebrew education for young people, as well as for adults. It became the cultural arm of the Zionist organization in Canada.

Fundraising activity to help develop the Israeli economy broadened considerably. New organizations were founded to foster trade between Canada and the Jewish state, and corporations were formed to promote capital investment in Israeli industry and the sale of Israel bonds. Both Zionists and non-Zionists participated in all these activities.

An organization with the name Canada-Palestine Corporation (Canpal) was created to establish trade links between Canada and Israel. This company, under the leadership of its national president Mr. Barney Aaron, aided in the development of trade relations between the two countries, which have increased annually. Subsequently more companies were formed to encourage investment in the State of Israel.

With non-Zionists also very involved in collecting large sums of money for Israel, either through the sale of Israel bonds or by soliciting on behalf of the United Israel Appeal, the differences between Zionist and non-Zionist Jews have diminished for all intents and purposes. This often raises the question as to whether the Zionist Organization is still necessary. One frequently hears, particularly from Zionists, that the Zionist movement is in crisis and that non-Zionists have taken over Zionist work, leaving Zionists with little to do.

In fact, Zionist leaders are now very busy defining the specific goals of organized Zionism. At Zionist meetings—conventions and seminars—this issue is always on the agenda and debated at length. The practical answer given by Zionist leaders is that organized Zionists have a more profound understanding of the needs and problems of Israel and that they are working—or should be working—toward the creation of a Hebrew culture to link the Jews of Israel with the Jews in the Diaspora.

There are also Zionists who are unconcerned about this so-called crisis. On the contrary, they take pleasure in seeing non-Zionists so excited and enthusiastic about fundraising for Israel. They believe this sort of "crisis" to be indicative of the revitalization and reinvigoration of Jewish national consciousness, to be a sign of Jewish unity, and not of decline. They consider it fortunate for all Jews that the State of Israel has won the support of both non-Zionists and assimilated Jews apparently alienated from their Jewishness.

Organized Zionists, however, are understandably more worried about the future. They wonder about the next generation removed from the dramatic events which marked the Jewish world during our lifetime. Will successive generations be as influenced by Israel as we are today? This question is not as prevalent in non-Zionist circles, even those involved in the large fundraising campaigns for the State of Israel.

In the meantime the Zionist organization has huge responsibilities. Apart from fundraising, there is cultural and educational work to be done, as well as public relations. It is up to the Zionist movement to protect Israel's reputation and honour from overt and covert enemies who could potentially harm the Jewish state.

The Labour Zionist and the Mizrahi movements are preoccupied with their own specific projects on behalf of the State of Israel. Certain activities are community-wide and carried out in concert through the United Zion Council. The president of the general Zionist organization, Joseph Frank, is the president of the United Zion Council.

Historic Jewish Anniversaries

Milestones Highlighting the Historic Character of the Canadian Jewish
Community. The Fundamental Values Uniting All Sectors of the Jewish
Community.

THE JEWISH COMMUNITY in Canada today is firmly established. Most Jews are
now Canadian-born and well integrated in the life of the country both
economically and culturally. The historic milestones celebrated over the last
few years reflect the fact that the Jewish community in Canada already has a
long past.

In 1959 the Canadian Jewish Congress proclaimed a full year of celebration
to commemorate 200 years of Jewish life in Canada. This anniversary was
observed in all the Jewish communities of the country. Jewish settlement began
in 1760 with the first Jew to come to Canada, an officer in the British army
who arrived when the British conquered Quebec. While Canada was a French
colony, there were no Jews here.

A second important anniversary of historic proportions occurred in 1918,
the 150th anniversary of the first synagogue in Montreal, the Spanish and Portuguese Synagogue (She'erith Israel), built in 1768. The Spanish and Portuguese
Synagogue was founded by Jews whose families had fled Spain and Portugal
to Holland, Belgium, or England whence their descendants had emigrated to
Canada. Here they founded the first synagogue, and laid the foundation of
religious Jewish life in this country.

The second oldest synagogue in Montreal, the Sha'ar Hashamayim,
celebrated its 100th anniversary in the mid 1940s. The first members of this
synagogue were mostly German Jews, and for a long time it was called the
"German shul".

For a long time there were only Spanish[240] Jews in Montreal. At the
beginning of the 1800s German Jews fleeing the political unrest in Germany
and Austria began to arrive. Life under the despotic regimes of that era was
especially difficult for Jews.

Most German and Spanish Jews assimilated into the non-Jewish population. Their assimilation was inevitable since, apart from synagogues, parents had created no institutions or activities to keep their children connected to Judaism. The children lived in a Christian atmosphere and married Christians. The congregations they founded were eventually taken over by Eastern European Jews who brought to Canada not only religious doctrine but also a tradition which bound them to the vital Jewish life in Europe.

Both historic synagogues, the Spanish and Portuguese and the Sha'ar Hashamayim, are now frequented by Canadian-born Jews whose ancestors were from Russia, Poland, or Rumania. Even the rabbis are no longer descended from Spanish or German Jewish families. In the Spanish synagogue the spiritual leader is Rabbi Dr. Solomon Frank, who was brought here from Winnipeg. The spiritual leader of the Sha'ar Hashamayim Synagogue, Rabbi Wilfred Shushat, is from a Montreal family and a former pupil of the Montreal Talmud Torahs. When he took up his position in 1946, a year after graduating from the Jewish Theological Seminary, he was one of the youngest rabbis in the country.

Yet another important anniversary occurred in the summer of 1963. This was the 100th anniversary of the Baron de Hirsch Institute in Montreal.

The history of the Baron de Hirsch Institute mirrors the history of the organized Jewish community in Montreal. Created in 1863, it was the first Jewish social and philanthropic association in Montreal, the first institution from which the organized Jewish community subsequently developed. A committee under the chairmanship of Mr. Horace Cohen, whose father, grandfather and uncle had been intimately involved in the leadership of the community,[241] was in charge of the celebrations. At a dinner at the Queen Elizabeth Hotel, representatives of the provincial and federal government were among the guest speakers.

These anniversaries symbolize the fact that the Canadian Jewish community is no longer young but mature enough to have its own tradition and history. On the other hand, the community is not yet strong enough spiritually and culturally to be able to stand alone. Its spiritual strength derives from its connection to Jewish communities in other countries, especially the State of Israel.

Before the Jewish state was proclaimed, the Land of Israel was of interest mostly to Zionists. After the birth of the Jewish state, Israel became a concern for all Jews and a significant part of all community activity. Without this focus, there would have been a spiritual void that would have hastened the natural assimilation process.

Despite its diversity, the entire Jewish community of Canada is strongly united in helping the development of Israel in every respect. In the 1950s Canadian Jews invested large amounts of money in the Jewish state and this has continued in the 1960s. In the fall of 1951 the two major organizations, the Zionist Organization under the leadership of Lawrence Freiman and the Canadian Jewish Congress under the direction of Samuel Bronfman, created a united organization for investment in Israel. Thus the entire Canadian Jewish community became closely involved in the future of the Jewish state. In the spring of that same year, a large delegation of Canadian Jews flew to Boston to meet Prime Minister David Ben-Gurion who was then on a visit to the United States. In Boston's Somerset Hotel several dozen Canadian Jewish leaders assured the Prime Minister of Israel of Canadian Jewry's fullest support.

Changes in Jewish Life

The New Jewish Community in the Suburbs. The Problems of Integration and
Assimilation. The Role of the Synagogue. Many Questions and Few Answers
Concerning the Future.

SOON AFTER the Second World War, it became evident that a transformation
was taking place in the life of the Jewish community. New economic, cultural,
and social realities were dictating the future course of Jewish activities on the
national as well as the local level. World War II brought prosperity and a higher
standard of living for the majority of Canada's population. Construction
projects were initiated in cities and towns, creating a real estate boom and the
proliferation of large apartment buildings and shopping centres. Jewish entre-
preneurs got involved in this activity, many of them becoming very successful.

Then began the trend to build new suburbs. Jewish families were among
the first to move away from the centre of the large, bustling metropolis to
enjoy fresher air, more space, and better facilities. The process of relocation to
the suburbs occurred in all cities, large and small, in both Canada and the
United States.

In these suburbs new expensive modern synagogues were built along with
large community centres for young people and halls for celebrations and
parties. In the new synagogues one rarely, if ever, encounters a *heymish* rabbi
from the old country ordained in Slobodka, Telz, or Volozhin. The new rabbis
speak English, the everyday language of the members of the younger generation
who are unfamiliar with the Eastern European Jewish culture of their grandparents.

In the new suburban community there is little room for the organizations
and institutions created by the Yiddish-speaking Eastern European Jews of
previous generations. Now the main concern of these organizations is how to
attract the youth for whom Eastern Europe never had much relevance,
especially now, after the disappearance of its densely populated Jewish centres
and the destruction of its intensive cultural and religious life by the Nazis.

The youth of the new suburban community are mostly students. Jewish young people are a significant proportion of the student population in colleges and universities. Very few of them still enter the labour force as factory workers. The Jewish working class, very prominent in the 1920s and 30s, has become significantly smaller. In the large clothing factories where just a few generations ago Jewish workers were in the majority, there are now only small groups of Jewish artisans, and even they are becoming increasingly rare.

About the young students of today there is much debate. Will they be able to assume the burdens and responsibilities of the Jewish community in the future? Will they have anything in common with Jewish communities in other countries? Will they maintain cultural and economic ties with the Jews in the State of Israel?

These questions have become increasingly topical. They are often the subject of meetings and forums, national conferences and conventions. There is a prevailing fear that the rapid integration process among young students is distancing Jewish youth from Jewish national and cultural activities.

In statistical surveys, the Canadian Jewish Congress reports that about 50 percent of Jewish school-aged children receive no Jewish education. What will happen when these children grow up and have children of their own? How will their Jewishness find expression? And for those children who do enjoy a Jewish education, how long can it remain effective in the university atmosphere where the influence of scientific knowledge is so pervasive?

In the Jewish community a few decades ago Yiddish culture flourished and created a sense of Jewish national identity and ethnic consciousness. This culture is now very weak, barely recognizable. And what is taking its place? For the time being, nothing at all. What will fill this void? For certain Jewish writers and intellectuals this vacuum is a bad omen. They see it as a symptom of decline and a cause for grave concern. Others believe this to be an inevitable process, not a sign of decline or crisis but only of change, a change to which we must adapt. The void will be filled with other Jewish cultural values which will be created in another language in other forms more in tune with the new realities.

The general prestige of the Jewish community has grown considerably thanks to the existence of the State of Israel. The community is very generous in its support of the Jewish state. Non-Zionist groups participate in the fundraising campaigns on behalf of Zionist causes. But when Israeli leaders call for *aliyah*,[242] when Ben-Gurion says that Israel requires one million Jewish immigrants from America for its security, the response is not warm. On the contrary, he is criticized for demanding heavy sacrifices from American Jewish youth. Even certain Zionists contend that it is not realistic to make such demands in light of the fact that Jews in America and in Canada enjoy security and prosperity. They are under the impression that this prosperity is permanent. But is this really so? Can we be certain that the current affluence of the suburban Jewish community is any more secure than the economy of the country as a whole, which is beset by problems such as automation, unemployment, and inflation?

In the newly transformed suburban community synagogues are being erected on almost the same basis as large commercial enterprises. All that is required is a decision by a few Jewish citizens to build, and a costly synagogue with a huge annual budget is constructed. The expenditures, however, cannot be met by the congregants themselves or generated by religious functions. Revenue must be raised mainly by renting out halls for weddings, bar mitzvah parties, and so on. Although the synagogue's directors work on a volunteer basis, they must nevertheless treat the synagogue as a business venture. Instead of concerning themselves with the true purposes of the synagogue—prayer, study, education of children—they must expend most of their energy and effort on the commercial aspects in order to be certain of an income. The modern synagogue is therefore becoming more an institution for the middle class and well-to-do. The poorer sectors of the population cannot be accommodated there, even those who are observant.

Every Saturday there is a large bar mitzvah celebration in the suburban synagogue, and occasionally two or even three on a single Saturday. Teaching the *Haftorah*[243] has become the main goal of Jewish education. The bar mitzvah boy is showered with gifts and heartily congratulated at a lavish party. He is told that until now he was free of Jewish responsibilities, but as of today he is an adult who will have to bear the yoke of Judaism like all adult Jews. But the average boy feels otherwise. From his perspective, it is exactly the opposite. While he was young he had to attend a Jewish school, to study the *Haftorah* and other subjects. But from this day forth he is an adult, and, like all the other adults, like his father and his older brothers, he is now free. No longer must he attend the Jewish school. If he wants to, he can quit.

The changes in Jewish life have elicited many questions from thoughtful Jews. For the time being there can be no definite answers to these questions. They are closely related to the questions of Jewish survival and continuity and are often debated by rabbis, journalists, and intelligent community leaders concerned about the Jewish future.

These same issues have become timely in almost all the countries of the Diaspora. Canada, of course, is no exception. One can say with certainty that the situation would have been much worse were it not for the impact of the State of Israel which has affected all the diverse elements comprising the Jewish people.

The existence of Israel is therefore important not only for the Jews who live there, but also for Jews all over the world.

Montreal, 1964. A group of aging Yiddish writers discuss Jewish
survival and continuity in a changing world.
(From left to right) Israel Medres, Melekh Ravitch, and Mordecai Ginsburg.

Notes to Translator's Introduction

[1] The book was originally published as *Tsvishn Tsvey Velt Milkhomes*, literally *Between Two World Wars*, by the Eagle Publishing Co. Ltd, 4075 St. Lawrence Blvd., Montreal. The Yiddish reviews were written by Dr. Joseph Kage, Dr. Benjamin Orenstein (July 5, 1964), Yehuda Zilberman (in *Dos Vort*, the official publication of the Labour Zionist Movement of Canada, Vol. XVIII, No. 4, June 1964), and N. I. Gottlieb writing in the *Keneder Adler*.

[2] See, for example, Joseph Kage's article entitled "Able and Willing to Work: Jewish Immigration and Occupational Patterns in Canada," in M. Weinfeld, W. Shaffir, I. Cotler, *The Canadian Jewish Mosaic*, Toronto: Wiley, 1981.

[3] For example, Joseph Kage *Two Hundred Years of Jewish Immigration to Canada* [in Yiddish], Montreal: The Eagle Publishing Company, 1960; David Rome, in his multi-volume Canadian Jewish Archives series quotes repeatedly from Medres' articles.

[4] Israël Medresh, *Le Montréal juif entre les deux guerres*, Sillery: Septentrion, 2001.

[5] David Homel, "Pierre Anctil et les mémoires de monsieur Medresh", *La Presse*, February 3, 2002, page B1.

[6] Louis Corneiller, "Être juif à Montréal dans la tourmente", *Le Devoir*, February 23, 2002, page D5.

[7] As his granddaughter, I know that Medres seldom spoke about his early years. His family knew very little about his boyhood in the Russian Empire, about the parents and siblings he left behind. In his Lexicon of Jewish writers and artists, Melech Ravitch wrote that Medres was "*a Lechevicher landsman*, a native of Lechevich, but only according to the documents. In his heart Israel Medres was a Montrealer who had grown up with the Jewish community of Montreal." When he died, there was an outpouring of grief, and from the many obituaries I was able to glean a few details about his childhood. Other information came from articles about him on his sixtieth birthday, reviews of his book, and two of his own articles in the *Keneder Adler*. One is a 1953 review of the memorial book about his birthplace Lechevich. That book, *Lahovits: Sefer Zikaron*, contains much information about the town in the years that Medres lived there, between 1898 and 1910, including descriptions of the several elementary schools, *heders*, that Medres attended and the teachers who taught him. The other was part of a series of reports from Argentina which he visited in 1960 to be reunited with a sister who had been only a baby when he left for Canada. A letter from the government of Canada indicates that in 1928 Medres was attempting to bring a younger brother to Canada from Baranovich, then in Poland. Like hundreds of thousands of such applications it was rejected. This tragic episode, all too familiar to his contemporaries, is not included in *Between the Wars*.

[8] For historical background on the Pale of Settlement and the Jews of Russia, as well as Israel Medres, see my Introduction to Israel Medres, *Montreal of Yesterday*, Montreal:

Véhicule Press, 2000.

[9] In the book *Sefer Lida* ("The Book of Lida"), Tel Aviv, 1970, an article beginning on page 131 describes the classes in the yeshiva and the rabbis who taught the students in the years that Medres was there.

[10] The Poalei Zion movement began in Russia toward the end of the 19th century promoting an ideology of socialist Zionism. After the 1905 Revolution the movement spread to North America and in 1907 a World Union of Poalei Zion was founded. In 1920 the movement split with the Left Poalei Zion favouring affiliation with the Third International (the Comintern). However, by 1924 the Left Poalei Zion reorganized itself on an independent basis, while the Right Poalei Zion merged with the Zionist Socialists (Z.S.) in 1925, and in 1932 joined with the Histadrut in founding the World Labor Zionist Movement. See Chapter 9, "Labour Zionism".

[11] David Rome, *On Our Forerunners—At Work*, Montreal: National Archives Canadian Jewish Congress New Series No. 10, 1978, p.158, quotes the following from Irving Abella and David Millar, eds., *The Canadian Worker in the Twentieth Century*, Toronto: Oxford, 1978, page 201: "Leah Roback, an education worker for the I.L.G.W.U. recalls that as late as 1937 it had set up Sunday morning classes for Jewish cutters and pressers. 'And we had a very dear man. He was a writer for the *Jewish Daily Eagle*, and he was the labour reporter. He went from union to union. This man was an honest man and a man who understood the political situation in the province as well as the trade union movment—he understood it very well.' " David Rome has identified the man who lectured as Israel Medres.

[12]This story was related to me by David Augenfeld of Montreal. Mordecai Ginzberg (1894-1966), also a prolific staff writer for the *Keneder Adler*, arrived in Montreal in 1930 after writing in Vilna, Lodz and Brest-Litovsk.

[13] See David Rome, *The Yiddish Theatre: The Adler*, Canadian Jewish Archives New Series, No. 38, Montreal: National Archives Canadian Jewish Congress, 1987, pages 75-6.

[14] Yehuda Zilberman, *Dos Vort*, op.cit.

[15] Joseph Gallay, in an article written on the tenth anniversary of the death of Israel Medres.

[16] "I am pained to observe at this period so critical for our future, when we feel a patriotic awakening in our midst, that so much energy is being devoted, possibly the largest measure of activity, towards destroying each other. We must defend our positions, but we must not deprive others of the right to live." *Jewish Morning Journal* [*Morgn Zhurnal*], August 4, 1965, quoted in David Rome, *Clouds in the Thirties*, Section 1, page 37.

[17] Orenstein.

[18] "Reading Medres is essential for anyone interested in the question of anti-Semitism in Canada," wrote David Homel in *La Presse*, op.cit.

Translator's Notes to Text

[19] The *nom de guerre* of Vladimir Ilyich Ulyanov (1870-1924) was Nikolai Lenin. He has since become known as V. I. Lenin.

[20] Born Lev Davidovich Bronstein, Leon Trotsky (1879-1940) was the son of a well-to-do Jewish farmer in the Ukraine. As Bolshevik war commissar he built up the force which eventually became the Red Army.

[21] Anton Ivanovich Denikin (1872-1947) was commander of the anti-Bolshevik forces in southern Russia from 1918 to 1920. Simon Petlura (1879–1926), Ukrainian nationalist leader, was held responsible for not having stopped the wave of pogroms in the Ukraine in 1919 and 1920.

[22] Baron Piotr Nilokayevich Wrangel (1878-1928) in 1920 succeeded General Denikin in command of the counter-revolutionary White Army. Aleksandr Vasilyevich Kolchak (1872-1920), commander of the Russian Black Sea Fleet in World War I, organized the anti-Bolshevik government in Siberia which, though recognized by the Allies, was short-lived (1918-1919).

[23] Literally, the Land of Israel, as opposed to the State of Israel which was created in 1948.

[24] (1874-1952) In 1920 he became the leader of Zionism, and in 1948 first president of the State of Israel. In World War I he created a synthetic acetone needed by Great Britain for the manufacture of explosives. See Chapter 11, "Zionism after the Balfour Declaration".

[25] (1859-1936) Zionist leader, influential Hebrew journalist and prolific author.

[26] November 14, 1915.

[27] (1856-1946) American jurist and first Jew to sit on the U. S. Supreme Court.

[28] (1872-1937) American Jewish author, journalist and Zionist leader, he was the American Jewish delegate to the Versailles Peace Conference in 1919.

[29] (1867-1935) Hebrew and Yiddish writer, rabbi and Zionist leader. He represented Vilna in the first Russian State Duma of 1906 and later settled in Palestine.

[30] (1874-1960) A member of the Conservative party, he was Prime Minister in 1920-1921 and in 1926.

[31] (1858-1920) Member of an illustrious Sephardic family which settled in Montreal in the mid-19th century, he served as Belgian consul in Montreal from 1904-1920. See Israel Medres, *Montreal of Yesterday*, pages 20, 110-111, 160.

[32] (1889-1956) One of the founders and organizers of the Canadian Zionist Organization of which he was vice-president. A brilliant lawyer, he was influential in the Conservative Party and eventually was elected to the Quebec Legislature as a representative of the Union Nationale. He played a major role in the controversy over

the Jewish Schools Question. See Chapter 12, "Controversies in the Community", Chapter 28, "Fascism vs. Democracy", and Chapter 35, "The First Jewish War Immigrants".

[33] Born 1882 in Lithuania, settled in Montreal in 1906. Lawyer and Talmudic scholar who, in the 1950s, became the president of the Canadian Zionist Organization and president of the Canadian Jewish Congress.

[34] Born in Lithuania in 1880, he emigrated to Montreal in 1908 where he became a prosperous businessman and active in the United Talmud Torahs of Montreal.

[35] (1899-1980) Born in Montreal, he was an active Zionist from his youth as president of Young Judea. After joining the Jewish Legion in 1918, he settled in Palestine.

[36] Hirsch (Harry) Hershman (1876-1955) Immigrating from Bukovina to Montreal in 1902, he became known as a socialist and community leader. He ran the first Jewish bookstore, helped found the Canadian Jewish Congress, the Jewish Public Library in 1914, and the Peretz School. (See *Montreal of Yesterday*, pages 55-56, 167, 178). See Chapter 13, "The Crash of 1929".

[37] See note 9 in Notes to Translator's Preface and chapter entitled "Labour Zionism".

[38] Zvi Hirsch Cohen (1862-1950) Emigrating from Eastern Europe in 1889, he became the unofficial chief rabbi of Montreal. For many years he was the chairman of the Council of Orthodox Rabbis of Montreal.

[39] (1868-1937) Clothing manufacturer, he owned Freedman and Company, one of the largest and most successful clothing firms. He was one of the founders of the *Jewish Times*, the first Jewish periodical in Canada, and president of the Baron de Hirsch Institute from 1908-12. In 1919, he became the first president of the Canadian Jewish Congress.

[40] Dr. Herman Abramowitz (1880-1947) Born in Russia, educated in the U.S. before becoming rabbi of Montreal's Sha'ar Hashamayim Synagogue in 1903.

[41] (1862-1939) Well-known Hebrew and Yiddish writer born in Byelorussia, he worked in Moscow, St. Petersburg, Berlin, Vienna, New York, Warsaw, and Lodz, before coming to Montreal in 1912 to become the editor of the *Keneder Adler*, the Montreal Jewish daily founded in 1907. From 1912 to 1916, when he returned to New York, he was active and influential in the life of the Montreal Jewish community. See Israel Medres, *Montreal of Yesterday*.

[42] See note 9.

[43] Born in Montreal in 1879, in 1911 he became the youngest barrister in Canada to be appointed King's Council. In 1916 he was elected to the Quebec Legislature as a Liberal from the Saint Louis riding, Montreal until his death in 1942. As a lawyer, he had a reputation as champion of the poor, the underprivileged and the workers.

[44] (1865-1943) Philosopher and essayist. Born in Russia where he was active as a socialist and Jewish nationalist. Elected to the first Russian State Duma of 1906, but could not take his seat because of his revolutionary past. In 1908 settled in New York and became active as a writer and speaker advocating Jewish nationalism, socialism and Yiddishism. See *Montreal of Yesterday*.

[45] Hannaniah Meir Caiserman (1884-1950) Born in Rumania, he emigrated to

Montreal in 1910 where he was active in the Jewish trade union movement and the Labour Zionists. He helped found the Canadian Jewish Congress and various other Jewish institutions.

[46] Julius Rosenwald (1862–1932) Merchant and philanthropist. He was born in Springfield, Illinois, the son of German Jewish immigrants. While contributing substantially to Jewish war relief during World War I and the postwar period, he pledged $6,000,000 to promote Jewish agricultural colonization in the Soviet Union. He served for many years as vice-president of the American Jewish Committee.

[47] In 1924, with Soviet support, the American Jewish Joint Agriculture Corporation ("Agro-Joint") was founded to serve as the agent for the Joint Distribution Committee of American Funds for the Relief of Jewish War Sufferers (popularly known as the JDC and the "Joint"), an organization founded in 1914 under the chairmanship of Felix M. Warburg.

[48] Samuel William Jacobs (1871-1938) Prominent lawyer and leading figure in the Montreal Jewish community, he served as president of the Baron de Hirsch Institute from 1912 to 1914 and was elected to the Parliament of Canada for the Saint Louis riding in 1917.

[49] Adherents of the Jewish Enlightenment, the *Haskala* in Hebrew, *Haskóle* in Yiddish.

[50] For a discussion of the Hebraists, see *Montreal of Yesterday*, pp 64-66, 137-38.

[51] Founded in Vilna in 1916, the *Vilna Troupe* moved to Warsaw where its 1920 production of An-Ski's *The Dybbuk* brought international fame.

[52] Theatre company founded in Moscow in 1917 as the first professional Hebrew theatre in the world, and now the National Theatre of Israel.

[53] (1890–1960) Born in the Ukraine, he became one of the most popular of the American Yiddish actors and founder of Yiddish Art Theater in New York.

[54] The famous play *The Dybbuk*, written by author and folklorist Sh. An-Ski (pseudonym of Solomon Zainvil Rapoport) (1863–1920) in both Russian and Yiddish, was first produced in Yiddish by the Vilna Troupe (1920), and then, in the Hebrew translation of Bialik, by the Habimah company in Moscow, Tel Aviv, and New York. Translated into many languages, *The Dybbuk* was also made into an opera and a movie.

[55] Pseudonym of Leivick Halpern (1886–1962), Yiddish poet and dramatist. His involvement in the Russian revolutionary movement led to years of imprisonment. Following a dramatic escape from Siberia he emigrated to the U.S. in 1913 where he began working in a sweatshop and as a paperhanger. Like his many other works, the play *Shmates*, written in 1922, deals with the theme of human suffering.

[56] (1890–1977) actor and director. Ben-Ami began as a child actor in his native Minsk, Byelorussia. After traveling with many Yiddish acting companies through Eastern Europe, he settled in the United States in 1912. Together with Maurice Schwartz, he founded the Yiddish Art Theater in New York in 1918.

[57] (1880–1948) Yiddish playwright and novelist born in Poland who eventually moved to the United States where he also wrote his famous romantic play *Grine Felder* [Green Fields] in 1923.

[58] (1862–1930) A German Jewish actor who emigrated to the U.S. in 1911, he appeared

for one season on the Yiddish stage before returning to performing in German and English.

[59] A *landsmanshaft* is an association of people from the same town or region in Europe formed for the purpose of providing its members with mutual aid, health and death benefits, and other fraternal services. *Landsmanshaftn* is the plural.

[60] The lower house of the Polish parliament.

[61] (1879–1970) Zionist and one of the main spokespersons of Polish Jewry between the two world wars, Gruenbaum was a member of the Polish *Sejm* from 1918 until 1932, where he was known for his outspokenness against the anti-Semitic policy of the Polish government. In 1932 he left for Palestine, becoming the first minister of the interior of the State of Israel in 1948.

[62] See note 41.

[63] Zigmond Fineberg (1863-1967) in 1911 founded the Hebrew Free Loan Association which by 1923 had lent up to $100,000 interest-free.

[64] The International Ladies' Garment Workers Union (ILGWU), founded in New York in 1900, became active in Montreal around 1907 and played a prominent role not only in the economic sphere, but in the social and cultural life of the immigrant Jewish workers.

[65] The Amalgamated Clothing Workers of America (ACWA) was founded in New York in 1914. In 1916 the Tailors' Union joined the Amalgamated Clothing Workers of America. See also Israel Medres, *Montreal of Yesterday,* p.142.

[66] The *Arbeiter Ring,* or *Arbeter Ring,* in English the Workmen's Circle, was a Jewish fraternal order founded in 1900 in the United States to provide its members with mutual aid, health, and death benefits, to support trade unions and socialism, and promote Yiddish culture. The Montreal branch was created in 1907. See *Montreal of Yesterday*, pages 45-47, 81.

[67] In the 1920s the split within the Workmen's Circle reflected the division over the question of affiliation with the Communist International (the Comintern or Third International), created in 1919. A group favoring communist ideology broke off to form the Labour League, a fraternal order known after 1945 as the United Jewish People's Order.

[68] The Histadrut, the General Federation of Jewish Workers in Palestine, founded in 1920 as a federation of trade unions, was involved in economic and cultural activities as well as mutual aid for workers. See Chapter 9, "Labour Zionism".

[69] The Jewish Labor Committee was a community agency founded in New York by a number of trade unions and other organizations in 1934 to support Jewish labour institutions in European countries, assist the victims of Nazism, and cooperate in combating fascism, Nazism and anti-Semitism.

[70] The Jewish Labour Bund was the abbreviated name of the General Jewish Workers' Union of Lithuania, Poland and Russia, a socialist party founded in 1897 which promoted the Yiddish language and secular Jewish nationalism while opposing Zionism.

[71] Prayer recited by a mourner.

[72] In 1917 the Talmud Torahs (Jewish religious schools) of Montreal had been united under one administration with Samuel Weiner as the first president.

[73] Hirsch Wolofsky (1876-1949) In addition to launching the *Keneder Adler* in 1907, Wolofsky was one of the founders of the Canadian Jewish Congress and a leader of the Jewish community in Montreal. See also Chapter 10, "Zionism After the Balfour Declaration", Chapter 22, "The Doctor's Strike Against the Jews", and Chapter 35, "The First Jewish War Immigrants".

[74] Literally, "City Council." See chapter, "Problems of Religious Jews".

[75] (1895-1986) A Montreal lawyer who ran as a Liberal candidate against the communist Fred Rose in the provincial elections of 1943.

[76] (1882-1968) Philanthropist who contributed to the Mount Sinai Sanitorium, the Jewish General Hospital, and the Y.M-Y.W.H.A., and administrator of the Canadian Jewish Congress.

[77] Became chairman in 1945.

[78] *Keren Hatarbut Ha'ivrit*, literally, the Hebrew Culture Fund. It raises money for Hebrew cultural activities.

[79] (1911-1997) Community leader, educator, and author of *Striking Root: Reflections on Five Decades of Jewish Life*, Mosaic Press, 1979.

[80] Those in charge of enforcing *kashruth*.

[81] See note 9, in Notes to Translator's Introduction.

[82] (1875–1971) U.S. trade union leader and journalist. Born in Byelorussia, he settled in the U.S. in the 1880s where he worked in the sweatshops of New York. Active in the revolutionary socialist labour party and the trade union movement, especially as secretary-treasurer of the Amalgamated Clothing Workers of America for the next twenty-five years, in 1940 Schlossberg resigned to devote his time to community and Zionist affairs.

[83] Abraham Isaac Shiplacoff (1877–1934) American labour leader born in Russia, emigrated to the United States in 1891. Shiplacoff was the first socialist elected to the New York State Assembly (1915–18).

[84] (1885–1959) Born in Russia, Zaritsky arrived in the U.S. in 1905 where he became active in the United Hat, Cap and Millinery Workers' Union, becoming president in 1919. A labour Zionist, Zaritsky later worked on behalf of unrestricted immigration to Palestine and an independent Jewish state.

[85] (1884-1963) Labour leader, scholar, and second president of the State of Israel (1952-1963).

[86] Shneur Zalman Shazar (Rubashov) (1889-1974) Scholar, writer, and socialist Zionist, third president of the State of Israel.

[87] (1887-1970) Labour Zionist leader. Born in Russia, immigrated to the U.S. in 1903 where he became one of the chief spokesmen of the Poalei Zion. He was also among the founders and promoters of the Farband, the Jewish Legion of World War I, the American Jewish Congress and the Histadrut Campaign.

[88] Golda Meir (Myerson) (1898–1978) Prime minister of Israel from 1969 to 1974.

[89] Jewish community in Eretz Israel (Palestine) before the establishment of the State

of Israel.

[90] The Union of Zionists-Revisionists was founded in 1925 and led by Vladimir Jabotinsky. It advocated a Jewish state with a Jewish majority on both sides of the Jordan River.

[91] Vladimir (Ze'ev) Jabotinsky (1880–1940) A Zionist activist, soldier, orator, writer, poet, and founder of the Jewish Legion during World War I, Jabotinsky greatly influenced a large section of the Jewish people. As head of the Betar movement, he inspired many thousands of Jewish youth, particularly in Eastern Europe. His oratorical skills, in Russian, Hebrew, Yiddish, English, French, and German, drew large audiences all over the world.

[92] See note 86.

[93] Sydney Webb (1858-1947) Together with his wife Beatrice (1858-1943), he helped build the British Labour Party and wrote numerous works on socialist history and theory. The Passfield White Paper issued when he was the British colonial secretary in response to the riots of 1929, aimed at severely restricting Jewish agricultural settlement in Palestine.

[94] (1881-1951) British trade union and political leader whose policy was to limit Jewish immigration to Palestine.

[95] (1890-1956) Arriving in Montreal from Poland in 1912, he was a teacher at the Folk Shule and worked as a journalist. He became co-founder of the Jewish Peoples Schools where he was a teacher. He was also one of the founders of the Poalei Zion in Montreal and the Canadian Jewish Congress.

[96] Isidore M. Bobrove Q.C. Lawyer and active Labour Zionist, he was one of the founders of the Canadian Jewish Congress, the Histadrut Campaign in Canada, the United Zionist Council, and Canpal Canadian Israel Trading Company Ltd., which he chaired for many years.

[97] Dr. Samuel B. Hurwich. A Toronto pediatrician and Zionist activist who was elected to the Actions Committee of the World Zionist Organization in 1960.

[98] Leon Kronitz. A graduate of the Kletzker Yeshivah in 1930 and Tarbut Teacher's Seminary in Vilna in1935, he came to Canada before World War II where he graduated from McGill and became a Jewish educator and active Zionist.

[99] Mapai, from the initials of Hebrew words *Mifleget Poalei Erez Israel*, known as the Labour Party, was founded in 1930 as a Zionist-Socialist party and soon became the dominant party in the Jewish community and the labour movement.

[100] Archibald Jacob Freiman (1880–1944) arrived in Canada in 1893 from Lithuania. He founded Freiman's Department Store in Ottawa, and from 1920 to his death was national president of the Zionist Organization of Canada.

[101] Lillian Freiman (1885–1940) was born in Mattawa, Ontario. From 1919 to her death she was president of Canadian Hadassah. She was involved in philanthropic and relief work for Jews as well as non-Jews, and in 1920–21 brought 150 Jewish orphans, survivors of the pogroms in the Ukraine, to Canada. See *Montreal of Yesterday*, p. 178.

[102] In Yiddish, *geule* (from the Hebrew) which can be translated as salvation,

deliverance, redemption, the coming of the Messiah.

[103] Acknowledged leader of American Jewry, delegate to the Versailles Peace Conference. See *Montreal of Yesterday*, page 175.

[104] The *Keren Hayesod* (Palestine Foundation Fund) was the financial arm of the World Zionist Organization, established in 1920 to raise funds to encourage immigration and colonization, and private business, in Palestine.

[105] Abraham Menahem Mendel Ussishkin (1863–1941) was one of the early Zionist leaders and president of the Jewish National Fund.

[106] *Keren Kayemet Leisrael* is the land purchase and development fund of the Zionist Organization founded in 1901 at the Fifth Zionist Congress at Basle.

[107] In Hebrew, *Emek Hefer*. This was the central part of the Sharon Plain between Haderah in the north and the Netanya-Tul-Karm road in the south. Initially 8,000 acres was acquired by the Jewish National Fund. This purchase, one of the largest at the time, was made with the financial assistance of Canadian Zionists.

[108] The Mizrachi (its name is derived from the Hebrew words *merkaz ruhani*, meaning spiritual centre) was founded in 1902 as a national-religious organization within the Zionist Organization by Rabbi Jacob Reines, whose yeshiva Israel Medres attended from 1907-10.

[109] (1839–1915) He was the first head of the Mizrachi movement. See *Montreal of Yesterday*, page 18.

[110] Rabbi Abraham Isaac Kook (1865–1935) in 1921 became the first Ashkenazi Chief Rabbi of Palestine.

[111] Rabbi Abraham Dov Shapira. The visit took place in May, 1924.

[112] (1866–1933) Renowned Talmudist, early Zionist and head of the Slobodka yeshiva in Kovno, Lithuania.

[113] The Mizrachi Organization of America was established in 1911 by Rabbi Meir Berlin (Bar-Ilan) (1880-1949), who settled first in the U.S. in 1915 and later in Palestine in 1926.

[114] Rabbi Judah Leib Fishman (1875–1962), known as Maimon, was also a leader of religious Zionism who played an active both role in Europe before 1913, and then in Palestine, becoming a cabinet minister in the first government of the State of Israel.

[115] See note 38.

[116] Rabbi Wolf (Ze'ev) Gold (1889–1956), one of the leaders of religious Zionism, emigrated in 1907 from Poland to the U.S. where he achieved renown as an orator and helped to establish various educational and communal institutions.

[117] Gedaliah Bublick (1875–1948) was a Yiddish journalist born in Eastern Europe who settled in New York City in 1904. An active Zionist, he was one of the founders of the American Jewish Congress and the Mizrachi Organization of America.

[118] The *Yidishe Tageblatt* (Jewish Daily News), the first Yiddish daily founded in 1885 in New York, was conservative, traditional and against socialism and atheism.

[119] Arriving in Canada at the age of 21, Mr. Sternthal became a Montreal businessman and served on the boards of many Jewish religious educational institutions as well as

the Jewish General Hospital and the Hebrew Free Loan Society.

[120] (1911–1996) Arriving in Canada in 1948 to be the director of the Mizrachi Organization of Canada, in 1960 he was instrumental in helping the Canadian Jewish Congress to obtain a law recognizing the Jewish ritual slaughter of animals as humane. For many years, Zambrowsky was chairman of the National Religious Welfare Committee of the Canadian Jewish Congress.

[121] This situation existed in the Province of Quebec only.

[122] See note 32.

[123] (1879–1942) Born in Montreal, Bercovitch, a lawyer and King's Counsel, was elected in 1916 as a Liberal in the Quebec Assembly, thus becoming the first Jew to have a seat in the provincial legislature where he served seven consecutive terms. In 1923 he was largely responsible for defeating a bill designed to deprive Quebec's Jews of equal public school rights, arguing the case before the Privy Council in London, but he opposed separate schools for Jews. He also served in the House of Commons, was the first president of the Jewish Immigrant Aid Society and honourary vice-president of the Canadian Jewish Congress.

[124] Louis-Alexandre Taschereau (1867-1952) was the Liberal Premier of Quebec from 1920 to 1936.

[125] See note 38.

[126] See note 41.

[127] The transcripts of the debates of the Legislative Assembly with regard to Jewish Schools were published as a separate book in 2001 by the Service de la reconstituiton des débats, Bibliothèque de l'Assemblée nationale, Quebec. 17th Legislature – 3rd and 4th sessions, March 28 to April 4, 1930 and February 24 to April 4, 1931.

[128] See note 66.

[129] See note 36.

[130] (1871-1925) Social Democrat and first president of the Wiemar Republic (1919-25).

[131] (1865-1939) Social Democrat and first chancellor of the Weimar Republic. He resigned over the Treaty of Versailles.

[132] Erich Ludendorff (1865-1937) German general who took part in Hitler's Munich beer-hall putsch, 1923.

[133] Paul von Hindenburg (1847-1934), German field marshal and president. With Socialist help, he defeated Hitler in the presidential elections of 1932, but in January of 1933 was persuaded to appoint Hitler as chancellor. He continued as a figurehead until his death.

[134] See note 130.

[135] See note 133.

[136] Gustav Stresemann (1878-1929), German chancellor (1923)and foreign minister (1923-29), who attempted to secure a respected place for Germany by fulfillment of its treaty obligations and conciliation of its former enemies. He signed the Kellogg-Briand Pact (1928) for which he shared a Nobel Peace Prize with Aristide Briand, the French foreign minister.

[137] Both the Dawes Plan (1924), named after the American Vice-President, Charles G. Dawes, and the Young Plan (1929), named after Owen D. Young, were designed to reduce German reparation payments to the Allied Powers and stabilize German finances.

[138] German chancellor (1930-32), leader of the Catholic Centre Party, who passed unpopular drastic financial decrees and dissolved Hitler's storm troops in 1932. He was dismissed by President Hindenburg who appointed Franz von Papen as his successor. Franz von Papen was instrumental in bringing about Hitler's appointment as chancellor in 1933.

[139] (1899-1967)

[140] The Protocols, an anti-Semitic forgery claiming a worldwide Jewish conspiracy to enslave or kill non-Jews, was widely circulated during the Russian civil war by opponents of the Bolshevik Revolution, and contributed to the extensive pogroms perpetrated in southern Russia between 1918 and 1920. They were introduced to the West by Russian émigrés fleeing the revolution, becoming most popular in Germany, even before the rise of Hitler.

[141] The Nazis Joseph Geobbels (1897-1945) and Julius Streicher (1885-1946) were Hitler's chief propagandists.

[142] The pornographic and anti-Semitic periodical edited by Julius Streicher.

[143] (1890-1959) Lawyer and founder of the Union Nationale Party in 1935, he served as Premier of Quebec from 1936-39 and again from 1944-59.

[144] Henri Lemaître Auger (1873-1948) subsequently was elected to the Quebec Legislature, and eventually became a cabinet minister in the Duplessis government. His motion tabled in the City Hall called for prohibiting the immigration from Germany, Russia and Central Europe of refugees "professing communist and anti-Christian ideas" as the most effective way of combating unemployment and preserving "Christian traditions" in Canada.

[145] Henri-Adonai Quintal represented the Sainte-Marie Ward from 1921 to 1934.

[146] (1889-1952) Schubert served as general secretary of the Montreal Section of the International Ladies Garment Workers Union from 1916-1926, alderman for the Saint Louis District from 1924 to 1940, and first chairman of the Joint Commission of the Men's and Boys' Clothing Industry from 1935 to 1952. See *Montreal of Yesterday*, pages 140 and 144.

[147] Alderman for the Laurier District from 1930-60.

[148] Alderman for the Saint Lawrence District from 1931-34.

[149] See footnote 123 for information on Peter Bercovitch.

[150] Joseph Cohen, of the law firm Cohen and Gameroff, served as a Liberal member of the Quebec Legislature from 1926-35. See pp. 76-78.

[151] See note 123.

[152] Samuel William Jacobs (1871-1938) Prominent lawyer, president of the Baron de Hirsch Institute from 1912 to 1914, elected to the Parliament of Canada for the Saint Louis riding in 1917. See Chapter on "The Attack on the Talmud" in *Montreal of Yesterday*.

[153] See Maurice Paléologue, *La Russie des tsars pendant la Grande Guerre*, Paris, Plon, 1922, vol. 2, p. 36.

[154] He is referring here to the Dreyfus case in France and the role played by Edouard Drumont. See *Montreal of Yesterday*, p.122.

[155] For the text of this judgment see David Rome, *Clouds in the Thirties, On Anti-Semitism in Canada 1929-1939*, Section 2, Montreal, 1977, and The Canadian Jewish Chronicle, September 16, 1932.

[156] See note 150.

[157] Grandson of Louis-Joseph Papineau, Henri Bourassa (1868-1952) was first elected to the Parliament of Canada in 1896 as a Liberal. From 1908-12 he served in the Quebec Legislature where he was leader of the powerful nationalist opposition party. He again served in the Federal Parliament from 1925-35.

[158] Louis-Joseph Papineau (1786-1871) Elected to the Legislative Assembly of Lower Canada in 1809, he became speaker of the legislative assembly of Lower Canada (1815-37) where he fought for democratic reform. His followers, the *Patriotes*, led the 1837 Rebellion against the British Government of Lower Canada.

[159] In 1832 legislation was enacted in Lower Canada giving full civil rights to Jews, including the right to sit in the Legislature and the right to hold public office. The full text of Mr. Cohen's speech delivered on February 16, 1932, can be found in the *Débats de l'Assemblée legislative*, p. 657.

[160] Montreal daily newspaper published by Olivar Asselin. See note 163.

[161] Journalist and editor of *Le Canada* from 1934 to 1937 and from 1942 to 1947.

[162] Israel Rabinovitch (1894-1964) Noted musicologist and writer, Rabinovitch joined the staff of the *Keneder Adler* in 1918, and was its editor-in-chief from 1924-64.

[163] Olivar Asselin (1874-1937) A Quebec nationalist known for his enlightened views and his stance against anti-Semitism. See Michael Oliver, *The Passionate Debate*, Montreal, Véhicule Press, 1991.

[164] See note 45 and Chapter 21, "The Creation of the Second Canadian Jewish Congress". In an article which appeared in the *Canadian Jewish Chronicle* on February 25, 1938 entitled "Canadian Jew-Baiting on Exhibition", Medres described an exhibit organized by the Canadian Jewish Congress featuring "a motley collection of anti-Jewish journals, leaflets, books, and pamphlets which are being circulated in Montreal and throughout Canada." ".... Even in anti-Semitism," writes Medres, "there is a lack of uniformity." Some of the publications, including Arcand's papers, as well as German imports and those printed in Ontario and "points further west", seem to be competing "as to which can emerge the victor in literary sewage," employing the "foulest pogrom language". A second category was the economic branch of anti-Semitism, including "Achat Chez Nous". A third class of anti-Semitism was that of the Church. The "defence" side of the exhibition was in the form of replies prepared by the Congress, i.e., by Mr. Caiserman. In response to them, and several "good will" conferences between the Congress and the Catholic clergy, "theological anti-Semitism has diminished during the past few years." But "Achat Chez Nous" was still around, and the English circular "Boycott the Jew" was "another bulky piece of material which had gone the rounds in

Ontario," along with a pamphlet "Why we should oppose the Jews?," the latter two apparently part of a "large importation" from other countries, the bulk of them from Germany."

[165] See note 48.

[166] See note 45.

[167] Dr. Samuel Rabinowitch.

[168] The strike took place on the nights of June 14 and 15, 1934, and spread to the other francophone hospitals, from the Hôtel Dieu to the Misèricorde, Sainte-Justine, and Saint-Jean-de-Dieu hospitals. Those who had instigated the strike were members of Jeune Canada. See Michael Oliver, *The Passionate Debate, The Social and Political Ideas of Quebec Nationalism*, 1920-1945, Montreal, Véhicule Press, 1991, pp. 189-90

[169] See note 55.

[170] Medres is referring to the Amalgamated Clothing Workers of America and the International Ladies' Garment Workers' Union (ILGWU).

[171] By 1931 almost three-quarters of all gainfully employed Montreal Jews worked in the clothing industry. See Louis Rosenberg, *Canada's Jews: A Social and Economic Study of the Jews in Canada in the 1930s*, Morton Weinfeld, ed., Montreal and Kingston: McGill-Queen's University press, 1993, page 365.

[172] (1893-1975) Russian-born labour activist and member of the Poalei Zion who later became a city alderman from 1940-42.

[173] Born in Russia in 1890, emigrated to the United States in 1906 where he became active in the ILGWU in 1909. From 1929-31 he was a union organizer in Toronto, and in 1934 arrived in Montreal from Chicago as an organizer for the ILGWU. In 1950 he became the Vice-President of the ILGWU. See Chapter 37, "Immigrant Tailors from the D.P. Camps".

[174] The strike took place in April and May of 1937. See Gerald Tulchinsky, *Branching Out, The Transformation of the Canadian Jewish Community*, Toronto, Stoddart Publishing Company Limited, 1998.

[175] Tissot was fined $50. However, Mr. Justice Kelly of the Ontario Court stated that he had "known no other case of public prosecution where the initiation of the prosecution had been so severe," adopting the view that Tissot was indeed "a martyr of over-vigorous prosecution by the Jew Freiman." David Rome, *Clouds in the Thirties: On Antisemitism in Canada 1929-1939*, Section 2, Montreal, Canadian Jewish Congress, 1977.

[176] Rabbi Bernard Mednick, rabbi of the Quebec City synagogue Beth Israel Ohev Shalom from 1937-1945.

[177] (1885-1968) Arriving in Canada from the Ukraine in 1902, Maurice Pollack settled in Quebec City where he founded the city's largest department store and generously supported Jewish institutions in Canada and Israel, as well as Canadian institutions such as Laval University.

[178] In 1930 Sam Factor, a Liberal, was elected for Toronto West-Centre (later called Spadina).

[179] Abraham Albert Heaps (1885-1954) was elected to Parliament as a member of the Independent Labour Party from 1925-40, and later as a member of the C.C.F.

[180] Joseph Maurice Scott.

[181] Rabbi Harry Joshua Stern (1897—1984) Born in Lithuania, Stern was brought to the United States as a child. From 1927 until his death, he was the rabbi of Temple Emanu-El in Montreal, the first Reform Congregation in Canada. Besides his activities in the Jewish community and Zionist movement, he was committed to the ecumenical movement and wrote books on Jewish-Christian relations.

[182] See note 143.

[183] See note 32.

[184] Seenote 159.

[185] Member of the Liberal party and Premier of Quebec from 1939 to 1944.

[186] Liberal M.L.A. representing the St. Louis Ward from 1939 to 1947, and federal Member of Parliament from 1947 until his death in 1950.

[187] Archibald B. Bennett (1891-1980) Historian, journalist, and one of the founders of the Canadian Jewish Congress, Ontario Region in 1919.

[188] Tisha b'av: the 9th day of the Hebrew month of Av, a day of fasting to mourn the destruction of the temples in Jerusalem.

[189] Lawyer, chairman of the Jewish Immigrant Aid Society in 1928, and honourary vice-president of the Canadian Jewish Congress from 1939-60.

[190] Dr. Herman Abramowitz (1880-1947) Born in Russia, educated in the U.S. before becoming rabbi of the Sha'ar Hashamayim Synagogue in 1903. See *Montreal of Yesterday* regarding his role in the Montreal Jewish community pre-World War I.

[191] See note 181.

[192] Camillien Houde (1889-1958) A former Quebec M.L.A. and Mayor of Montreal from 1928 to 1954, he was interned from 1940 to 1944 for his opposition to conscription. See next chapter.

[193] Anti-Jewish statutes proclaimed in September 1935 at the National Socialist National Convention in Nuremberg stripping Jews of their German citizenship and forbidding marriage or sexual relations between Jews and German citizens.

[194] See note 24.

[195] The National War Efforts Committee was formed in late 1940. See Gerald Tulchinsky, *Branching Out*, pages 205-214.

[196] Philip Madras, youngest son of Israel and Sophie Medres.

[197] Tilburg.

[198] From another letter written by Philip Madras to his parents and printed in the Canadian Jewish Chronicle, November 3, 1944: "For the past two years, these people, like other Jews, were kept in hiding, in cellars, in attics, in barns, anywhere...When the Germans were finally beaten these people came out of hiding. For some of them it was the first time in two years that they saw actual daylight, and breathed fresh air. Of course, only a small proportion of the community was able to find shelter, the others were taken away by the Germans. Just what has happened to any of them, is not known...Of a family of nine, including two children, the parents, and aunts and uncles, only one was left..."

[199] Lend-Lease was the U.S. policy adopted in 1941 to provide arms, raw material, and

food to countries at war with the Axis powers. According to the Library of Congress website (http://lcweb.loc.gov) about $11 billion in war materiel was sent to the Soviet Union under that program.

[200] The Jewish Anti-Fascist Committee along with four other "antifascist committees" —for youth, scientists, women and Slavs—all supervised by the Ministry of Foreign Affairs, was formed in 1942 to assist the Soviet war effort by influencing public opinion at home and abroad and enlisting foreign support for the war effort through personal contacts with Jews in other countries. The committees were all disbanded by 1948.

[201] Solomon Mikhoels (1890-1948) was considered the greatest Soviet Yiddish actor, one of the founders and director of the Moscow Yiddish State Theatre and chairman of the Jewish Anti-Fascist Committee. In May of 1943 he and Itsik Feffer were sent to the United States and Canada for on a seven-month tour to enlist aid for the Soviet war effort. He was murdered on Stalin's instructions in a car "accident" in Minsk in 1948.

[202] (1900-1952) Soviet Yiddish poet who became the chief spokesman for the Communist Party line in Yiddish literature. Arrested in 1948, he was killed along with the other members of the Jewish Anti-Fascist Committee in 1952. Recently the transcript of the trial of the members of the Jewish Anti-Fascist Committee has become available to scholars and confirmed that Feffer had been an informer for the Soviet secret police. The transcript, as well as an account of the events surrounding it, are included in *Stalin's Secret Pogrom: The Postwar Inquisition of the Jewish Anti-Fascist Committee*. Edited by Joshua Rubenstein and Vladimir P. Naumov. Translated by Laura Esther Wolfson. New Haven: Yale University Press, 2001.

[203] Their visit to Montreal was on September 6 and 7, 1943.

[204] (1906-1980) A Montreal lawyer, he was the executive director of the Canadian Jewish Committee for Refugees before becoming the executive director of the Canadian Jewish Congress from 1940-59, and vice-president of the C.J.C. from 1959-74.

[205] Michael Garber (1897-1977) One of the founders of the Canadian Jewish Congress and president from 1962-68.

[206] See note 73.

[207] See note 123.

[208] During World War II, Jews with German or Austrian citizenship were placed in internment camps in Canada, including the camp at Ile-aux-Noix.

[209] The initials of this organization are from the Russian language since it was founded by prominent Russian Jews in 1880 to foster vocational training and cooperative workshops for Jews. By the 1930s ORT schools had been established throughout Europe, North and South America, and Australia.

[210] Dudley Leigh Aman (1884-1952), created Baron Marley in 1930, was a member of the British House of Lords and chairman of the Parliamentary Advisory Council of the ORT. As president of the Relief Committee for the Victims of German Fascism, in 1933 he issued a report entitled "Child victims of Hitlerism" and wrote an introduction to the "The Brown Book of Hitler Terror and the Burning of the Reichstag", published in the same year. In 1934 he authored the report *Biro-Bidjan: An Eye-Witness Account*

of the New Home for the Jews about the attempt to create a Jewish autonomous region in the far eastern region of the Soviet Union.

[211] David Lvovich (1882-1950) Vice-Chairman of the ORT World Federation from 1921, after World War II he organized occupational training projects in the Displaced Persons' camps of Europe.

[212] Founded in 1914 to provided relief to the Jews of Eastern and Central Europe and Palestine.

[213] See note 45.

[214] (1910-2000) Born in Radom, Poland, he came to Canada in 1927 where he became a member of the Communist Party and editor of the *Vochenblatt*, a Yiddish-language party organ, for twenty years. After breaking with the party in 1957, he remained very active in the Toronto Jewish community, particularly as a champion of the Yiddish language.

[215] The UJPO was a Jewish communist organization, with branches in Montreal, Toronto, Hamilton, Windsor, Vancouver, and Winnipeg, which promoted distinctly Jewish as well as left-wing causes.

[216] (1883-1957) From 1922-39 a deputy in the Polish parliament, the *Sejm*, he briefly served in the provisional government of liberated Poland before immigrating to the U.S. in 1946.

[217] See note 33.

[218] Hermann Wilhelm Goering (1893-1946) founder of the Gestapo, he invented the slogan "guns instead of butter".

[219] This chapter was reproduced in a volume entitled *Antologia: La Literatura Idish de Canada*, published in 1974 in Buenos Aires, YIVO, part of a 100-volume set of the masterworks of Yiddish literature edited by Samuel Rollansky.

[220] See note 173.

[221] The functions of the Jewish Agency for Israel were outlined in Article IV of the British Mandate over Palestine which recognized the Zionist Organization as that agency. Before the establishment of the State of Israel in 1948 it was responsible for advising the British administration of the interests of the Jewish people in Palestine and of "matters as may affect the establishment of the Jewish National Home."

[222] See note 106.

[223] See note 104.

[224] See note 68.

[225] (1894-1965) Head of the Jewish Agency's political department in 1933, he was among its leaders interned in 1946. After 1948 he went on to play a leading role in the State of Israel.

[226] David Remez (Drabkin) (1886-1951) Active in the labour movement in Palestine, he later served in the government of the State of Israel.

[227] See note 35.

[228] See note 61.

[229] (1898-1969) Labour leader in Palestine who became a member of the Israeli parliament, the Knesset (1941-51), and later the mayor of the City of Haifa (1951-69).

[230] See note 114.

[231] David Ben-Gurion (Green) (1886-1973) became Israel's first prime minister.

[232] (1891-1952) Became minister of finance of the State of Israel.

[233] See note 90.

[234] Clandestine organization for Jewish self-defence in Palestine which became the nucleus of the Israeli army.

[235] See note 93.

[236] See note 94.

[237] See note 186.

[238] (1921-1944) Budapest-born poet Hannah Szenes went to Palestine in 1939 and in 1943 volunteered for the British army.

[239] In 1954.

[240] Descendants of the Jews expelled from Spain in 1492, known as Sephardim. See *Montreal of Yesterday*, pp 37-39.

[241] See *Montreal of Yesterday*.

[242] The immigration of Jews to Israel.

[243] Haftorah is a chapter from the Prophets read in synagogue each morning following the reading from the Torah.

Index

129
Histadrut 45, 47, 135
Horowitz, Rabbi Aaron 39-40
Houde, Camillien 106, 112
Hungary 84
Hurwich, Dr. Samuel 47
Hushi, Aba 135

Immigration 9, 70-72, 124; Canadian
  government policy 124, 131-32
International Ladies Garment
  Workers Union 132
Irgun 135, 138
Israel: creation of the State 143;
  relations with Canada 144

Jabotinsky, Vladimir 46-47
Jacobs, Bernard (Dov Joseph) 22
Jacobs, K.C., Leon W. 27
Jacobs, S.W. 73, 84, 96-97
Jewish Agency 135, 141
Jewish Anti-Fascist Committee 121-
  22
Jewish Immigrant Aid Society 125-26
Jewish Labor Committee 36
Jewish National Workers' Alliance 44
Jewish Public Library (Montreal) 31
Jewish War Efforts Committee 114
Jewish Workers' Committee 132-34
Joint Commission of the Cloaks
  Industry 89

Kaplan, Eliezer 135
Karen Hatarbut 39-40, 52, 144
Karen Hayesod 135
Karen Kayemet 50, 135
Kashruth 42-43

Keneder Adler (Jewish Daily Eagle)
  10-12, 38, 50, 59, 73, 79, 87, 102,
  118, 122, 141
Kook, Rabbi Abrahm Isaac 52-53
Kronitz, Leon 48
Kuhn, Fritz 83

L'Action Catholique 94
La clef du mystère 68, 99
Labour Zionists and Zionism 10, 25,
  44-48, 59, 89, 141, 145; Actions
  Committee 47-48;
Lambert, Dr. Gabriel 68, 99
Lavery, Salluste 69, 96
Lazarovitch, Sydney 95
Le Canada 79
Le Devoir 76-77
Le Fasciste canadien 98
Le Goglu 73, 75-77
Le Jeune Canada 83
Le Miroir 73, 75-77, 79
League for Christian Store Owners
  against Jews 92
League of Nations 66, 82, 109
Lenin, Nikolai 18-19
Lida Yeshiva 52
Lipschitz, Samuel 128
Lithuania 26
Litvinoff, Maxim 109
Locarno Treaty 66
Lvovich, Dr. D. 125

Maisel, Chaim 52
Mapai party 48
Marley, Lord 125
Marshall, Louis 49
Marxists and Marxism 30, 122-23